FAMOUS
FINANCIAL
FIASCOS

*

Richard Whitney

FAMOUS
FINANCIAL
FIASCOS

BY JOHN TRAIN

ILLUSTRATIONS BY *Pierre Le-Tan*
FOREWORD BY *C. Northcote Parkinson*

Clarkson N. Potter, Inc., Publishers
DISTRIBUTED BY CROWN PUBLISHERS, INC.,
NEW YORK

Text copyright © 1985 by Bedford Research, Inc.
Illustrations copyright © 1985 by Pierre Le-Tan

"Mr. Ponzi and His Scheme" and "The Putrefaction of Juan March" were first published by *Harvard* Magazine.

Published by Clarkson N. Potter, Inc., One Park Avenue, New York, New York 10016 and simultaneously in Canada by General Publishing Company Limited

Manufactured in the United States of America

Designed by Karen Grant

Library of Congress Cataloging in Publication Data

Train, John.
    Famous financial fiascos.

    1. Speculation—History.   2. Finance—History.
3. Swindlers and swindling—History.   I. Title.
HG6005.T73   1984   332'.09   84-14754
ISBN: 0-517-54583-7

10 9 8 7 6 5 4 3 2 1

First Edition

CONTENTS

*

FOREWORD

In TIMES PAST THE SOCIETIES MOST PRODUCTIVE IN enterprise, invention, and thought have been those in which the efforts of the successful and the rewards given to them have been very nicely balanced indeed.

But there has always been at least one exception: the success due to mere chance, the luck of the draw, the fall of the cards, the monarch's favor, the lottery's result. As a further exception there has always been, and there still remains, the fortunate investment: the purchase of something at what turns out to be a fraction of its value. Wealth gained by chance is usually lost by chance, the winning gambler being a gambler still. Sometimes, however, we attribute to luck what was actually an example of intelligence, forethought, and care. The author of this important book has taught us a great deal about investment; enough to show us that the handling of capital is both a science and an art. The element of luck remains, however; the earthquake, the invasion, the drought, and the epidemic. But things more often go wrong as a result of mistakes made. In this volume the able and painstaking author has usefully analyzed a number of these human errors and we do well to study his conclusions. Some of the worst mistakes have been made by people to whom the nature of their problem was entirely new. They lived at a time when the textbooks of economics had still to be written, at a time when the word "inflation" was applied only to balloons. There are still such people today and they can be identified, very often, as folk who have plunged into industry without any previous background in commerce. It is not for them, however, that this book has been written. It was planned, rather, for people who live in a highly developed society, for people familiar with economics; for people, nevertheless, who are still prone to financial catastrophe.

There are three typical causes of disaster of which we should all be aware. First of these is the confusion of purpose. In the foundation and development of a successful enterprise there must be a single-minded pursuit of financial profit. Bring in some other motive, admirable though it may be in itself—the desire to provide employment, the wish to bring prosperity to a poor district, the gaining of prestige for one's country, the urge even to provide evidence to support some favorite religious, political, or economic dogma—and our whole effort has from the outset a probably fatal defect. For one thing, our success or failure is not subject to arithmetical proof. For another, we have added confusion to a problem which should be relatively simple. Here is the basic flaw in the nationalization of industries: the injection of emotion into what should be a mathematical equation. An additional weakness may result from the recruitment of managers whose doctrinal orthodoxy may be more evident than their competence or drive. In matter of business we do well, in general, to stick to the point.

A second cause of possible disaster lies in overgenerous investment, the overcapitalization of ventures which may be sound in themselves. It is difficult in the nature of things to provide a sufficient return on a needlessly massive investment. Up to a certain point the injection of capital produces good results. Beyond that point the whole process goes into reverse. And remember that reckless expenditure of the first venturers will be copied and exceeded by the later executives. No one will ever have said, in so many words, that expense is no object. That message is implicit, rather, in the height of the head office building and the size of the purely administrative staff. People in general understand the value of what they personally have, beyond which figure they are lost. When figures under discussion become astronomic, 1 million and 2 million look alike, neither figure meaning anything. Accountants may know what they are talking about, but they can be easily outvoted by people who surpass them in imagination. When the organization is overstaffed, the problem is not one of work being done twice but of work wholly neglected, everyone having left everything to everyone else.

A third cause of disaster results from a mistake in timing. A good idea can be put forward some fifty years too late. A still better idea can be advocated some twenty years too soon. Even five years either way can be fatal. What fails to sell in Y year is successfully marketed by our rivals in Y + 5. Where public demand is involved our foresight needs to be uncanny; the more so in that the planning process may take up the time during which the product should have reached the market. In public speaking much of the art—half of it, as some would say—is in timing. The story told by A amid tumultuous applause meets with a stony silence when told by B. The words may be the same but the pauses are wrong, the moments of silence misplaced. So it is on the bigger stage of industry or commerce. Suppose we have set aside all wishful thinking and learnt, perhaps the hard way, that big expenditure is no certain recipe for a big success. We have still to decide *when*. This may well be the moment when the business consultant comes into his own—not that he is infallible but because he is not personally involved. It is easy to say afterward "We were too late on the scene" or "We were too quick on the draw," but the lesson to be learnt is far from elementary. Our tendency, next time, is to do the reverse of what we did before, each mistake being followed by its opposite.

In this volume the reader will find, clearly explained, where other men have gone wrong. From it we can learn when the commonest mistakes have been made, resolving not to repeat them. It is better to learn from a book than to learn in a bankruptcy court. Lessons learned are not always easy to apply, but readers of this excellent work should learn and apply at least one lesson: the lesson of humility.

C. NORTHCOTE PARKINSON

FAMOUS
FINANCIAL
FIASCOS

*

Mr Ponzi and his Scheme

MR. PONZI AND HIS SCHEME

A PROPER AMBITION OF EVERY YOUNG AMERICAN
of ability and zeal is to give his name to something big: to become eponymous. With what a fine, grim smile must our first
president, reposing on a celestial alabaster throne and enve-
loped in a toga of clouds, hear a hundred million taxpayers ex-
coriating *Washington;* how disconcerting for Union General
Hooker to survive only because of the bad girls that swarmed
about his headquarters (described as "half barroom, half
brothel"); and how pleasantly ironic that the *Teddy* Roosevelt
who brandished the Big Stick, scattered the Spaniards, grabbed
the Canal, and extinguished whole herds of African animals
should be remembered by that cuddly toy, the teddy bear.

But few malefactors leave a name behind them. Dillinger,
Capone, Joe Bananas, where are they now? The last person one
thinks of in connection with "Jamesian" is Jesse James. So in the
pantheon of crime Charles Ponzi, of the *Ponzi* scheme, enjoys a
secure niche.

Italian-born as Bianchi, later Ponsi, he started in Montreal
around 1907 near the bottom of the ladder of iniquity as a modest con man in a firm that helped his fellow Italians arrange

1

their remittances back to loved ones in Napoli and Palermo. Many of us have had occasion to find out what an eternity international money transfers can take. The banks collect interest on the idle balances, so they are happy for the transaction to drag out. In this narrow area of finance Bianchi/Ponsi was a *petit maître:* his transfers were conducted at so stately a pace that many have not arrived to this day, three-quarters of a century later.

Then there was the rubber-check imbroglio. A year later the Canadian authorities, apparently misunderstanding some technical detail, actually stuck Bianchi/Ponsi in prison for forging signatures on a series of checks. On his reemergence into the light of day our hero resolved to lead a new life. Not to go straight, of course, but to do things differently . . . better. Shaking from his boots the dust of Montreal—and its courts and its jails—he headed south, to Boston, town of the bean and the cod. But the path to success is arduous. Before he could devise his big coup Bianchi/Ponsi, now rechristened Charles Ponzi, tried washing dishes . . . hard on the hands and dull; running his in-laws' agricultural produce business . . . bankruptcy; clerking in an import-expert firm . . . tiresome and complicated.

While promoting a loose-leaf periodical for people in the import-export trade he wrote to acquaintances abroad, and in August 1919 received an answer from Italy. Inside the envelope nestled an International Postal Reply Coupon, redeemable in stamps. As Ponzi peered gloomily at the little square of printed paper he noticed a curiosity. The coupon had in fact been bought in Spain. Because International Postal Reply Coupons were redeemable at fixed rates of exchange negotiated by the participating governments, while currencies themselves can fluctuate wildly, this coupon had cost Ponzi's correspondent only one-sixth as much to buy in Spain as it was worth in stamps of the United States.

Well! Many of us have been struck by falling apples, but only Newton, rubbing the spot and glaring upward, derived the law of gravity. Just so, numberless correspondents must have noticed the Postal Reply Coupon anomaly, but only Charles Ponzi, on

that August day in 1919, saw in it the possibility of vast profits
. . . fraudulent, naturally.

Why couldn't you march into the post offices of some be-
nighted land whose currency had collapsed, acquire stacks—
bales, indeed—of these coupons for next to nothing, and thereafter, presenting them for redemption in a strong-currency
country, make an immediate, huge profit, in stamps? After that,
one would need only to wholesale the stamps, perhaps to business firms at a slight discount. The thing was a gold mine!

The first step was to form a firm, a sound, solid firm. A sound,
solid name suggested itself: The Securities and Exchange Company. Then, experienced, reliable officers and employees. As
president and, indeed, the entire staff, who better than Charles
Ponzi himself? A splendid start!

The deal offered by The Securities and Exchange Company
was irresistible. You handed over your cash, the S.E.C. worked
its wonders with the coupons, and after ninety days you got back
your original stake plus a profit of 40 percent. Very satisfactory
. . . particularly compared to the then prevailing interest rate of
5 percent or so.

The S.E.C.'s "prospectus" percolated around Boston in the
early weeks of 1920, and investors started to trickle in from here
and there, the way a few gulls and then more and more materialize when you toss some scraps out on the water. The initial investors were not turned out in black suits with ample waistcoats
anchored by gold watch chains; rather, coming mostly from
Boston's North End, they were the same simple immigrants that
Ponzi understood and had victimized in the past. A number of
policemen, themselves rather simple souls in financial matters,
signed up as customers.

Soon the word got about, and the inflow of cash picked up. It
became a torrent in February, when the S.E.C. lifted its rate on
ninety-day notes to 100 percent, and began offering a 50 percent
return on forty-five-day notes. Now the money began to pour in
so fast that President Ponzi scarcely knew what to do with it all.
Six clerks stacked piles of banknotes in closets until they scraped
the ceiling. Wastebaskets did duty as coffers for greenbacks. A

second office was acquired, and soon overflowed with money like the first. Crowds filled the street, waiting to turn over their savings for S.E.C. paper. Periodically they were treated to glimpses of the Midas himself, rolling up in his cream-colored Locomobile, complete with Japanese chauffeur. Ponzi—all five feet three inches of him—became a vision of opulence, his dapper raiment perfected by a malacca cane and a gold-tipped cigarette holder.

As the financial Niagara continued to pour, Ponzi acquired a quarter-share of the Hanover Trust Company. After that he took over J. R. Poole & Co., the import-export company where he had once been employed. He talked of opening branch offices . . . twenty, thirty. Also a chain of movie houses, a group of affiliated banks, even a steamship line.

The Boston papers were strangely silent on these exciting prospects. Finally, on July 26, the Boston *Post* broke silence. It ran an article claiming the whole thing was impossible: there weren't enough International Postal Reply Coupons sold to Ponzi to be doing what he claimed.

Some of the investors got the wind up. A number hastened to the S.E.C.'s offices in School Street to demand money for their notes. As fast as they appeared they were issued Hanover Trust checks paying them off in full, with interest. Ponzi appeared in person to pooh-pooh the problem. Observers were permitted a glimpse of a certified check for a million dollars languidly peeking from one pocket. The newspaper story was irrelevant, Ponzi assured the crowd. In reality he had quite a different method of multiplying the money, a wonderful method he had to keep secret for a time, for the sole use of The Securities and Exchange Company: the Postal Reply Coupon business was a decoy. The crowd was impressed, and the confrontation passed off satisfactorily. By the end of the day the S.E.C. had accepted another two hundred thousand dollars.

Then came trouble. The D.A. stepped in. Ponzi must desist from taking in new funds, pending an audit of the books. There was a run on the S.E.C. Policemen had to push people back into line. Several women collapsed. Some noteholders who irrupted through a glass door were lacerated by shards. The president appeared undismayed. His clerks went on writing Hanover Bank checks as fast as notes were presented. A Ponzi Alliance Organization promised support. Ponzi announced that he would use his profits to "do good for the people," and was cheered in the streets.

A week later the *Post* let fly again. This time it was an article by Ponzi's former publicity man, one William H. McMasters, who opined that Ponzi was "as crooked as a winding staircase" and in debt to the tune of some $4 million. Furthermore, asked McMasters, if the S.E.C.'s scheme really made its investors 50 percent in forty-five days, why did Ponzi himself put his own money in 5 percent bank deposits? And why had he scuttled out of the office one day to a store to take advantage of an offer of a free pair of shoes?

New crowds of agitated noteholders surged to School Street, to be soothed by more hundreds of thousands' worth of Hanover checks. More cheerful and confident than ever, Ponzi announced a $100 million worldwide investment syndicate. Declaring that he was being persecuted at the behest of the big bankers, he filed a $5 million suit against the *Post*. He and his wife were cheered in their box in the theater.

August, though, was bad. The Massachusetts State Banking Commission closed down that helpful institution, the Hanover Trust. And the *Post* sniffed out Ponzi's earlier career in Montreal, the aliases, the disappearing transfers, the bum-check rap, the stretch in the pen. There was even a Canadian mug shot, minus the gold-tipped cigarette holder.

Then the auditors revealed that the whole operation was an absurdity. After token transactions of merely $30, Ponzi had never used the International Postal Reply Coupon idea at all. He simply paid off earlier investors with funds received from later ones. There was no network of international correspondents. The S.E.C. was at least $3 million in the red.

The roof fell in. Using the mails to defraud, conspiracy, grand larceny, bankruptcy, civil suits. Once again, Ponzi was hustled to the slammer. But the legal uproar continued unabated, and his time behind bars was enlivened by constant expeditions to court to testify at one hearing or another.

Let out on parole after three and a half years, Ponzi was rearrested, jumped bail, fled to Florida under an alias, and was sentenced to jail there for real estate fraud: he was promising 200 percent profit in sixty days. He again jumped bail, was recaptured, and disappeared into a Massachusetts jail for seven years. On emerging, he was deported to Italy, got a job at Alitalia in Rio de Janeiro, was sacked when Alitalia closed down there during World War II, ran an unsuccessful boardinghouse, taught English, and finally died in a Rio charity ward.

He had worked on several books, but the publishers, as usual, missed their opportunity. One was called "The Rise of Mr. Ponzi"; another was called "The Fall of Mr. Ponzi."

THE PITS: CONTI READS ITS OWN ADS

ONE OF THE LARGEST COMMODITY BROKERAGE houses, ContiCommodities, a subsidiary of Continental Grain, for years ran huge ads in the newspapers that, in a subtle reverse pitch, printed descriptions of "mistakes" that commodity speculators were prone to make. The ads described types of speculators who should not enter this market (as though any should), and listed "rules" for doing well (as though this was even remotely likely). Here are some of the company's admonitions:

• "Keep reminding yourself on every position you take, 'My first loss is my least loss.'"

• "Do not overstay a good market—you are bound to overstay a bad one also."

• "Most people would rather own something (go long) than owe something (go short); it's human nature. The markets aren't human. So you should learn that markets can (and should) be traded from the short side."

• "Recognize that fear, greed, ignorance, generosity, stupidity, impatience, self-delusion, etc., can cost you a lot more money than the market(s) going against you, and that there is no fundamental method to recognize these factors."

- "Don't blindly follow computer trading. A computer-trading plan is only as good as the program. You know the old saying, 'Garbage in, garbage out.' "

Very nice! Unfortunately, someone in ContiCommodity believed their own ads. The company set up three commodity mutual funds, which were snapped up by an eager public.

All three lost so much money that they had to be closed down.

TULIPOMANIA

THERE SEEM TO HAVE BEEN SPECULATIVE BOOMS
and busts throughout history, such as those in saints' relics* and
in "unicorn" horns (actually narwhal tusks) to be made into
kings' goblets that neutralize poison. But the first extensively
documented one in Europe seems to be the early seventeenth-
century Dutch frenzy called *Tulpenwoerde*—tulip madness, or
tulipomania. At its peak, family fortunes were squandered for a
single bulb. It can serve as a perfect example in miniature of the
great speculative frenzies that have come since, including those
in our own time.

First, the tulip itself. The name may come from Turkish *dul-
ban*, a turban. In the mid-sixteenth century, travelers in Turkey
had been struck by the flower's beauty and had brought it to
Vienna; it soon attracted wide notice, and within a few years
was grown in Germany, then Belgium, then Holland. In the late
1570s it reached England, where the new flower became popular in court circles. Here was something new, interesting, and
valuable, on which public attention was understandably fo-

---

* Nine churches in France alone were able, at great expense, to acquire the foreskin of Jesus.

cused. It thus became a typical object of speculative interest. By the early seventeenth century in France, tulips were immensely fashionable, and the early traces of the later madness could be seen.

Cultivated tulips occasionally produce striking mutations, caused by a virus, which enhance their speculative interest. A grower would anxiously scan his garden for such a "break," as it was called; the bloom, then called "rectified," could, if beautiful, expect ready buyers, who would propagate and resell it at high prices, just as the sire of a Kentucky Derby winner today can command a huge figure from a stud farm. A yellowish stem base (called a "stained bottom") or a badly formed flower will be discarded; the perfect ones become "breeders."

By the early 1620s excitement over tulips and their mutations had reached Holland, and the rarest specimens were selling for thousands of florins. By degrees the madness spread from a handful of enthusiasts to permeate the whole of Dutch society. Soon virtually all houses had their tulip fields, filling every every inch of Holland's available surface.

Originally, sales occurred over the winter. A speculator might take some specimens and a supply of bulbs to one of the inns frequented by the confrerie of tulip traders. There he could exchange his "Admiral Tromp," purchased for five hundred florins, plus another two hundred florins in cash, for a "General Bol," which he would hope to sell within the week for a thousand. By 1634 every level of society had succumbed to this excitement, from laborers to the nobility, and soon deals were being conducted all year round, for delivery the following spring. What we call "put" and "call" options were invented and widely traded. Often the speculator had no intention of actually acquiring possession of what he had bought; rather, he expected to resell his contract promptly at a profit to some later enthusiast. This was called *windhandel*—trading air.

Tulips in seventeenth-century Holland presented even more problems than commodities today, since there was no member firm to stand behind the contract, and whoever finally did take delivery, often many months later, of a particular bulb could not

Tulipomania.

even be sure, until it actually bloomed, that he had received what the contract specified. To cope with this activity, new laws were promulgated, special tulip notaries were created, and special areas designated where the trade was to be carried out.

As the frenzy mounted, other economic activity slowed, and prices mounted giddily. Estates were mortgaged to permit their owners to participate in the constant rise of tulip prices; new buying power pushed prices up further. One "Viceroy" bulb sold for four oxen, eight pigs, twelve sheep, four loads of rye and two of wheat, two hogsheads of wine and four barrels of beer, two barrels of butter and half a ton of cheese, together with a quantity of house furnishings. A "Semper Augustus"—with vertical red and white stripes over a bluish inner hue—sold for about twice that value in cash, plus a carriage and horses. The Dutch became convinced that not only other Dutch speculators but also foreigners would pay ever-rising prices. Indeed, at one point a single rare bulb was given in France as full payment for a successful brewery.

One story illustrates the temper of those days. A shoemaker of The Hague, in the little plot that almost every Dutch household by this time had dedicated to tulip raising, finally managed to grow a black flower. He was visited by some growers from Haarlem, to whom he sold his treasure for 1,500 florins. Immediately one of them dropped it to the floor and stamped on it until it was ground to pulp. The cobbler was aghast. The buyers explained that they, too, possessed a black tulip, and had destroyed his to protect the uniqueness of their own. They would have paid anything: 10,000 florins, if necessary. The heartbroken cobbler is said to have died of chagrin.

But trees do not grow up to the sky, and the reckoning inevitably came. When these crazy price levels finally cracked, the entire economic life of Holland crumbled. Lawsuits were so numerous that the courts could not handle them.

Many great families were ruined, fine old merchant firms were thrown down, and it was years before commercial life in Holland recovered. The *Tulpenwoerde* had seared the Dutch soul, and in the centuries since there has been no recurrence.

THE FINAL SOLUTION TO PRUITT-IGOE

THE LE CORBUSIER THEORY OF LOW-COST HOUSING holds that workers' housing projects should consist of immense, symmetrical blocks of apartments, to replace the chaotic world of teeming, disorderly streets and packed four-story tenement buildings. The sleazy bars and their painted Lorelei, the funeral parlors, the banshee churches, the murky "social clubs" with their booze, drugs, and blackjack, all are to be subsumed into tall, clean, pure, antiseptic high-rise hives.

The Pruitt-Igoe project in St. Louis opened in 1955, designed along these principles by Minoru Yamasaki, architect of Manhattan's windy and sterile World Trade Center. Pruitt-Igoe consisted of thirty-three eleven-story slabs, deadly in their plainness. The elevators stopped on every third floor, which had an eleven-foot by eighty-five-foot gallery or "vertical neighborhood," in which, the architects hoped, children could play, bicycles could be stored, and the denizens could avoid the wicked streets outside, with their sweaty temptations. It was, in other words, a Salvation Army conception of housing. But these were not upper-crust tenants. Half were on relief, 98 percent were black, and of 11,000 occupants only 1,000 were adult males, since Missouri law forbids assistance for children to families with a father at home—which means that father moves out. But life isn't like that. The problem with those galleries, or "streets in the air," as Corbu liked to call them, is described by Tom Wolfe in *From Bauhaus to Our House:* "Since there was no other place to *sin* in public, whatever might ordinarily have taken place in bars, brothels, social clubs, pool halls . . . now took place in the streets in the air." The tenants were depressed by their dull, anonymous eleven-floor hives, but that was nothing to the more conventionally minded ones' shock and dismay at the goings-on in the public areas. They hated it. They left. As they departed, they were replaced by low-life elements, which made things even worse.

After ten years, *Architectural Forum* reported that:

The undersized elevators are brutally battered, and they reek of urine from children who misjudge the time it takes to reach their apartments. By stopping only on every third floor, the elevators offer convenient settings for crime. Every so often assailants will jam the elevators while they rob, mug, or rape victims, then stop at one of the floors and send the elevators on with the victims inside.

The stairwells, the only means of access to almost all the apartments, are scrawled with obscenities; their meager lighting fixtures and fire hoses are ripped out; and they too provide handy sites for predators. The breezeways at the entrances are hangouts for teenagers who often taunt the women and children and disturb those in close-by apartments with their noise.

The galleries are anything but cheerful social enclaves. The tenants call them "gauntlets" through which they must pass to reach their doors. Children play there, but they are unsupervised and their games are rough and noisy outdoor pastimes transferred inside. Heavy metal grilles now shield the windows, but they were installed too late to prevent three children from falling out. The steam pipes remain exposed, both in the galleries and the apartments, frequently inflicting severe burns.

The adjoining laundry rooms are unsafe and little used. They never served enough tenants to keep them continuously bustling with activity, and thus invited molesters. Now their doors are kept locked, and keys are distributed to the few tenants who use them. The storage rooms also are locked—and empty. They have been robbed of their contents so often that tenants refuse to use them.

What to do? You couldn't change the physical facts, so perhaps there was some way to run the project so that the more solid tenants would be less unhappy.

There followed eleven years of expensive studies, commissions, and task forces. The Public Housing Administration invested $7 million in improvements. Finally, in despair, the authorities assembled the remaining occupants of Pruitt-Igoe in a large hall and asked for their opinion of what to do.

Then and there, spontaneously, arose a great chant, crescendo: *"Blow it up! Blow it up! Blow it up! BLOW IT UP!"*

After a further year of pondering the alternatives, the authorities blew it up.*

* *There was a similar disaster in New Mexico, where a low-cost housing project for Indians was built in the form of high-rise apartments. The Indians, who depended on their gardens, detested them. Again, they were blown up.*

The Kuwait Stock Exchange explodes

THE KUWAIT STOCK EXCHANGE
EXPLODES

KUWAIT HAS BEEN RUN SINCE THE 1700s BY ABOUT twenty Sunni families who migrated there from the Nejd, in the heart of Arabia. One Nejd family, the al-Sabahs, ruled the country, to allow the others to make most of the money that there is to make. And when the oil boom came along, those families that were well installed in key businesses made very large amounts indeed.

The government pays for the education abroad of any qualified Kuwaiti boy. This has opened a social fissure in the country as non-Nejdi young men, mostly Shiites from the north, return from foreign studies feeling better prepared than their Nejdi counterparts, only to find their way to the top of the leading companies and ministries blocked by their ancestry. They became active in business anyway, and with the oil boom everybody prospered.

In 1980 these newly rich non-Nejdi Kuwaitis, who come right after the Lebanese as the keenest traders among the Arabs, discovered the joys of investing in the stock market. When the market had turned sickish in 1976 and 1977 the government had moved in to support prices, buying heavily for its own account, so that nobody would suffer. So the speculators looked at stock market investing like the gambling scene in *Fledermaus*, when it is announced that the prince will double the winnings of the winners and refund the losings of the losers.

Thus, when in 1980 the non-Nejdis started to put serious sums into stocks, and prices started to move, it was a coiled spring. Only a few dozen uninteresting companies were traded on the official exchange, so the unofficial market, or Souk al-Manakh, situated in an old structure once used for camel trading, became a cauldron of speculative activity, thronged with portly gentlemen in flowing white gowns (*thobes*) with capacious pockets full of papers, worry beads in one hand, cigarette in the other. Many plungers preferred to use their car telephones to trade while caught in one of Kuwait's dreadful traffic jams. Ramadan was the most active period, since everyone was so bored. It was pleasant to amble down to the al-Manakh after dinner and gamble until midnight or 1 A.M.

One Kuwaiti financial custom made a wild boom almost inevitable: well-established traders' postdated checks were accepted almost like cash. Legally, the payee could present a postdated check at any time, not only on the date written. But this was never done. It would have violated the old Kuwaiti tradition of trust, which also made it unthinkable that payment might not be made at all. A family simply had to make good on its commitments. There had, in fact, never been a bankruptcy. So when some stocks on the Souk al-Manakh began to jump 10 percent or 20 percent or even 50 percent a month, speculators rushed in to buy with postdated checks drawn against funds they did not have. They knew they could sell the shares to raise the cash when the checks came due.

Furthermore, buyers did not mind issuing checks dated in the future for double or triple the purchase price, convinced that quotations would rise that much by the time they had to pay.

So a market arose in postdated checks. Financial institutions hesitated to lend on shares, particularly queer companies on an unregulated exchange, but checks were fine—default was inconceivable.

This mechanism for creating buying power was gasoline on a fire: the market roared up. Soon new investment companies were formed to invest in other Manakh companies; there were even companies to invest in companies that invested in Manakh companies—a Fund of Funds of Funds, so to speak, each selling at large premiums over their assets. Many of the ultimate underlying companies were dubious speculations incorporated in Bahrain or the Emirates, subject to no regulation by Kuwait. Only about half of the Manakh companies even published annual reports. Entirely new ventures sold stock against postdated checks for several times the issue price; the checks could then be discounted—typically with foreign banks eager to break into the Kuwaiti financial scene—and the money applied to further speculation. It was a pure bubble. Legally, only Kuwaitis could trade, so all the Palestinian, Egyptian, and Pakistani lawyers, doctors, and accountants held stock through Kuwaiti nominees, leaving themselves without legal standing.

At the peak of the boom, in early 1981, some stocks were advancing 100 percent a month or more. A few went up ten times in 1980–81. Gulf Company for Industrial Development advanced fifteen-fold. The capitalization of the entire market soared from some $5 billion to perhaps $100 billion.

Kuwait is the financial center for the Arabian Gulf, so inevitably the frenzy spread. In nearby Sharjah, for example, there had some time before been a real estate boom as oil-rich local magnates put their profits into bricks and mortar, which they could see and touch. The failure of two banks had resulted in a collapse of the property market, and the magnates suddenly viewed their empty buildings with different eyes. The al-Manakh boom looked like a glorious chance to flog off a hundred-odd million dollars' worth of these structures, packaged as a public company. One of the most important components was a hotel that had been converted into a hospital, so the exciting name of Gulf Medical was devised for the assemblage. The stock was offered slightly below one dinar and was 2,600 times oversubscribed. For a whole week, one to two planeloads of completed subscription forms arrived daily from around the Middle East. The

National Bank of Sharjah, which was acting as subscription agent, couldn't cope with this volume of paperwork, and hired forty Egyptian school teachers to help out. Gulf Medical soared over 800 percent on the al-Manakh, and a lot of the magnates felt rich again.

A Little Matter of Being Temporarily Overdrawn

Some hyperactive speculators were able to push out *billions* of dollars of postdated checks. Eight individuals, called the Cavaliers, floated a total of $55 billion in checks, with the most energetic one, Jassim al-Mutawa, a Passport Office employee still in his twenties, passing off $14 billion all by himself. His brother, Najeeb al-Mutawa, didn't bother to record the checks he issued on the stubs in his checkbook. He thought they balanced, but when he finally totaled things up he found they didn't quite: he was $3.4 billion overdrawn. To troubled Western observers, Kuwaitis would say, pityingly, "You think of our market in terms of your own. But things are different here. Our government can't permit a collapse. Why tie up your money in something dumb like Standard Oil of Indiana when here you can make 30 percent a year?"

This explosion of credit could not be infinitely expanded. Three particular needles punctured the balloon. The first was the oil glut. The weakening of oil prices on top of lower sales meant that Kuwait's oil revenues in 1982 were only a quarter those of 1980. Then the new finance minister, Abdelatif al-Hamad, let it be known that he had no intention of supporting the market at the insane levels to which it had risen. Indeed, as it later emerged, he couldn't have even if he had wanted to.

Finally, on August 20, 1982, a jittery holder of one of Jassim al-Mutawa's postdated checks presented it for payment ahead of time—contrary to custom but conformably to law. Not surprisingly, the passport clerk couldn't pay. Bang! The balloon exploded. In no time hundreds of speculators were in default.

Collapse followed. Gulf Medical, for example, plunged about 98 percent to a sixth of a dinar.

In September, the Ministry of Finance ordered all doubtful checks to be turned in for clearance. Added up, they eventually came to over $90 billion, substantially more than Kuwait's total foreign reserves.

A vast brouhaha began at once. The old Nejdi families had generally remained aloof from the frenzy, but many government figures had participated in the wild ride, including, it was rumored, Minister of Commerce Jassim al-Marzouk, who was supposed to be regulating it. Some members of the ruling al-Sabah family were caught in the crash, and many members of Parliament. Since most of the aggressive speculators were non-Nejdi plutocrats, the old ruling oligarchy is determined to make the wealthier ones pay up at least in part, even if it means bankruptcy.

In the meanwhile, commerce has slowed to a trickle, and the fissure between the old Nejdi Sunni families and the rising new Shiite entrepreneurial class is deeper than ever.

GOVERNMENT

THE PRESIDENT'S PRIVATE SECTOR SURVEY ON Cost Control (also called the Grace Commission) reported in January 1984 that the General Services Administration, which operates government real estate,* employs seventeen times as many people, and spends fourteen times as much in overhead per unit managed, as a typical private-sector company managing comparable property.

The government owns a third of all the land in the United States, and occupies four times more office space than is found in our ten largest cities.

THE GREENER HILLS OF AFRICA:
THE GROUNDNUTS SCHEME

IT HAS FOR CENTURIES BEEN KNOWN THAT GOV-
ernment involvement is usually disastrous for agriculture. De
Toqueville notes that Montesquieu had long before made this
observation. The rule even applies to large corporations: our
West is littered with the cadavers of overambitious corporate
farming ventures that could not compete with the efficiency of
the large one-family farm—three to five thousand acres. There is
too much that must be known by one key man, too many rapid
decisions to be made, too much efficiency required, and the
work is too hard, to permit bureaucratization. Every farmer un-
derstands this, but few nonfarmers do. (Marx and Lenin were
nonfarmers: it is easy to see why Communist agriculture is
everywhere in crisis.)

England, in its idealistic fervor following World War II, succumbed for a while to the government agriculture heresy. The
Attlee Labour Government believed that the state should as-
sume many of the functions of private enterprise. When, therefore, it turned to the problem of England's margarine shortage,
and indeed the world postwar shortage of edible oils, it seemed
desirable for the government itself to undertake the solution.

There was plenty of unused land available in Britain's former territory of Tanganyika (now Tanzania), which also had a labor surplus. So the thing seemed a natural. As always, a commission was appointed, headed by John Wakefield, a Fabian socialist who had been Tanganyika's director of agriculture. In February 1947, after a three-month tour, his commission produced the Wakefield Report, entitled *A Plan for the Mechanical Production of Groundnuts in East and Central Africa.* (What Americans call the peanut is in England the groundnut.) Five thousand square miles of scrubland in the Kongwa and Urambo districts were to be cleared, roads and railroads built, thirty thousand Africans given work, valuable export earnings generated, the British and world shortage of margarine and cooking oil alleviated. Tanganyika would see the benefits of colonial rule; its people would remain contented and loyal.

John Strachey, Minister of Food, an Eton and Oxford ex-Marxist, relished the challenge of running a vast project. He established the Overseas Food Corporation to handle the job.

It was no easy matter. Not at all! For starters, bulldozers and tractors were in short supply. So in true swords-into-plowshares spirit, Sherman tanks were fitted up with blades and harrows and used in the fields: Hasn't everyone seen pictures of tanks pushing their way through underbrush, even bowling over small trees?

Now, your tank has many handy qualities under enemy fire, but it is heavier than the optimum tractor, immensely heavier, and uses vastly more fuel. Then, it is a most elaborate assemblage of machinery, requiring constant maintenance and overhauling by skilled mechanics, together with replacement of worn-out parts. The African bush is not richly supplied with either of those items. A Caterpillar tractor is less resistant than a tank to bullets, but is far preferable in all other applications.

Then, the vision of thirty thousand contented Tanganyikans hacking away at the undergrowth, saving up to send to Moss Bros. for black suits, bowler hats, and umbrellas so they could form circles and chant hosannas to their benefactor, John Strachey, proved unrealistic. The Tanganyikans had not been dis-

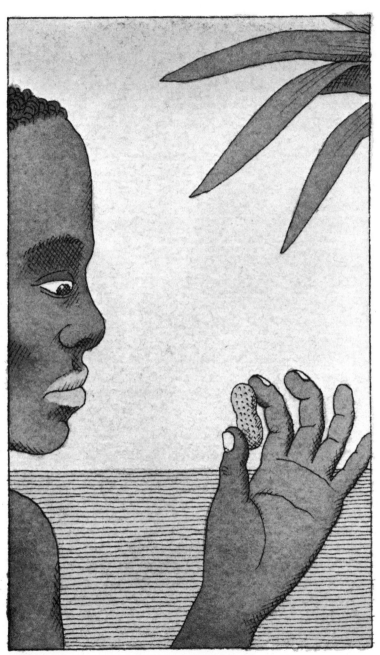

The Groundnuts Scheme

pleased with their former tranquil village life. So what if the right honourable gentleman considered them underemployed, not generating enough foreign exchange? What was he going to do as soon as he could afford it? Retire! So, they had *already* retired! Leave us alone! Strachey, vexed by this slack attitude, in essence drafted his laborers. Alas, draftees are not willing or effective workers. Thus, the Groundnuts Scheme's equipment and labor supply were scarcely of the first water.

In November 1948 Strachey annnounced that he was going to conduct an investigation.

A year and a half into the Scheme it was revealed that things were running a bit behind schedule: less than half of one percent of schedule, to be precise. And the auditors declared that they were "unable to report that proper accounts had been kept." Strachey announced to the House of Commons that the entire project would not be completed by 1949, but, reduced by a third, would be stretched out ten years.

By 1949 more than the original budget of £25 million had been committed, but the real farmers of the world had not been idle. Edible oil prices were falling. Locally, there was a severe drought. The auditors refused to certify the accounts. Something had to be done! A Commission of Enquiry was manifestly called for. After it had deliberated, the target size was further reduced, to 200,000 acres.

In 1950 it was noticed that there seemed to be a problem. A Working Party was assembled to study and advise. It established that the annual cost of producing £100,000 in crops came to £600,000.

Clearly, another investigation was needed! The Overseas Food Corporation conducted one later in the year. It found that for some reason groundnuts didn't grow well in that part of Tanganyika. Perhaps, however, Kongwa could become a cattle-ranching area.

Heavy rains, not contemplated in the original three-month Wakefield Report, now washed out the new railway. Thus ended any hope of exporting the few groundnuts that could be grown. The Groundnuts Scheme, extinct de facto, was officially buried by the government in January 1951. It had cost £36 million, only 50 percent over budget: no worse than the overruns of many projects . . . except, of course, that here there *was* no project any more.

All this was well noted by the electorate, and cost Labour heavily in the 1950 elections.

As to Minister Strachey, after this disaster—and, indeed, another, the disastrous Gambia Egg Scheme—there was only one thing to do and, courageously, the government did it. He was moved up, just in time for Korea, to the Ministry of War.

XEROX DISCOVERS THE COMPUTER:
THE S.D.S. DEBACLE

IN THE LATE 1960s XEROX CORPORATION DEVEL-
oped an intense yearning to get into computers. Its boss, Canadian lawyer and Harvard Business School graduate Peter
McColough, hungered and thirsted to get into computers. Con-
templating the office of the future, of which it wanted to be a
central part, Xerox realized that information, not the physical
copy, was the ultimate product. Information need not be stored
on paper. It can equally repose in the mind of a computer. You
then have to be able to find (or "access") it again, display or
print it for inspection, and transmit it to whoever needs it
next—perhaps by routing a copy to the next office, but also perhaps by reducing it to digital form and sending it out by wire or
satellite, on arrival to be displayed on a screen or turned again
into physical ("hard copy") form. So hard-copy technology,
where Xerox dominated, was crucial at the beginning and at
various later points, but you had to be able to slide in and out of
the computer en route. And indeed a big high-speed copier,
which is more powerful than a small newspaper press, needs its
own internal computer to help it work: what amounts to a skill-
ful, cheap, vigilant, nonunionized pressman.

So everything, Xerox felt, militated in favor of acquiring a computer capability. Then came the question, develop it internally, or buy it? The former was almost impossible. In a field growing that fast, you may start out strongly but never actually catch up. It's like Zeno's paradox of Achilles chasing the tortoise: every time Achilles gets to where the tortoise was, the tortoise has moved on, each time less, but still moved on. Except that the computer tortoise can suddenly speed up and start running like the wind. Indeed, it may run faster than Achilles. There is no presumption that a new computer company will ever reach the state of the art—which generally means IBM— on a broad front. Most times the new competitor makes its lunge but misses, and then never sees IBM again. And even worse is the terrifying amount of money involved, which turns this into a "bet your company" situation: giant enterprises like GE and RCA decided to go into computers, but after some years had to drop out of the game, financially exhausted by the insatiable cash requirements of the business.

No, the only realistic choice was for Xerox to buy its way in, for some specific, determinable amount, however large.

Fate, which stalks us all, now overtook Xerox, incarnated as Max Palevsky. The son of a Chicago housepainter, Palevsky had degrees in philosophy and mathematics. He tried teaching philosophy, but concluded he didn't have what it took to make a major contribution. Switching to business, he joined Bendix as a mathematician and found himself working on computers. He had an idea for a new approach, but the company wasn't interested. At Packard-Bell, in Los Angeles, he found support, and did in fact make and sell his own computer, but when he asked for a bigger piece of the action he was fired. He got backing from San Francisco venture capitalist Arthur Rock and others, and in 1961 started his own firm, Scientific Data Systems, taking Bob Beck from Packard-Bell to look after the technical side of the company.

By a happy circumstance both the space program and the silicon transistor had just arrived. So the market for scientific computers expanded at the moment the transistor made possible increased speed and accuracy.

S.D.S. boomed: $2 million in profits within three years, a

record that eclipsed even the older Digital Equipment Corporation.

By 1968 sales had soared to $100 million. By then, however, Palevsky and Beck had gotten out of their depth. Neither had big-company management experience. There were internal battles. Reorganization followed reorganization. Planning got further and further behind. Beck, by now a rich man, retired to his mountain ranch. Palevsky, also now a multimillionaire, became interested in film production, joined the Vietnam peace movement, and backed Robert Kennedy for president.

So when Xerox started looking around for an acquisition, S.D.S. was ripe. Digital Equipment and Control Data couldn't be bought, so S.D.S., the third choice, became the leading candidate. After much negotiation a deal was made on the basis of one share of Xerox for every two shares of S.D.S., now to be called Xerox Data Systems, or X.D.S. At Xerox's then share price, this was almost a billion dollars.

But almost half of X.D.S.'s business was still directly or indirectly tied to the space program. Soon after the acquisition the first astronaut landed on the moon. Since the computers needed for the program were already in place, the growth of that market could only decline.

Then came the 1970 recession. The whole computer market fell apart. Furthermore, the minicomputer was starting to eat into X.D.S.'s market. And within Xerox the corporate cultures of the computer people and the copier people proved to be incompatible. X.D.S. was a discount operation, while Xerox went first class in every sense. (When going by plane, everybody in Xerox, and essentially nobody in S.D.S., traveled in first.) It proved impossible to get neatly dressed, well-paid Xerox salesmen to downgrade themselves into disheveled, lower paid, price-cutting computer salesmen.

When X.D.S. lost $20 million in one year, Xerox chief Peter McColough put in his own man to run it. The losses continued. X.D.S. started falling farther and farther behind the market: Achilles losing ground to the tortoise. The minicomputer challenge intensified.

Finally the Xerox directors concluded that X.D.S. would never succeed. After a quarter of a billion dollars of operating losses on top of their billion-dollar acquisition, Xerox threw in the sponge and quit the business. Quite an expensive sponge, at that: a final after-tax writeoff of almost $100 million, after all the rest.

This was one of the most expensive bad deals in American business history. How did it happen? The euphoria of rising Xerox stock prices, the glamour of the computer field, the allure of the unfamiliar, sloppy homework, overoptimism, groupthink.

Max Palevsky, by now immensely rich, indulges his interest in left politics (e.g., George McGovern) and the American Civil Liberties Union, and in films, backing fellow-traveler movie-maker Costa-Gavras.

John Law in Venice at the end of his life

O MORE THAN MAN!
THE JOHN LAW SCANDAL

*

LOUIS XIV BLED FRANCE WHITE. HIS ETERNAL
wars, his colossal palace at Versailles with its unending enter-
tainments, the vast endowments he granted to his favorites, his
mistresses, and the royal bastards, these and a thousand other ex-
travagances devoured the wealth of his realm. He craved splendor, for himself as king in order to eclipse the outworn feudal
hierarchy, and for France, to establish it by the brilliance of its
arms and its arts as the first country of Europe. But splendor,
particularly military glory, costs immense amounts of money.
Even the indefatigable Colbert, who devised the centralized financial and administrative system that France has followed ever
since, could not satisfy Louis' insatiable needs for money. When
the king died, after seventy-two years on the throne, his successor, Louis XV, was only five years old, so the boy's uncle, Philippe, Duc d'Orléans, became Regent.*

With this title, Philippe inherited the problem of an over-
whelming debt: over 3 billion livres. There was no way to pay it

* *"The reign of Louis XV had begun. ... He had neither father,
mother, brothers, nor sisters; all had been killed by the wretched
Fagan."—Nancy Mitford,* Madame de Pompadour. *Dr. Fagan was
known as the "Killer of Princes."*

33

off; even the interest was an intolerable burden. What to do? National bankruptcy was considered.*

"Beau" Law—he had a solid face, a long, angled nose, and a square jaw—was a roistering Scottish gambler and dandy in the London of the last decade of the seventeenth century. In a duel with swords he killed another "Beau," Wilson, whose sister had insulted one of his many mistresses. Seized and convicted, he escaped from prison and fled into exile. As the son of a banker, he now turned his attention to public finance, and visited Amsterdam and other banking centers to study their financial institutions. In 1705 he published a tract entitled *Money and Trade Considered*, in which he argued that the more money in circulation in a country, the more prosperity it should enjoy. "Domestic trade depends upon the money. A greater quantity employs more people than a lesser quantity. An addition to the money adds to the value of the country." In today's language, inflation. At the time, "money" meant a limited supply of bullion in which debts such as government bonds, written on paper, had ultimately to be repaid. Law's objective was to induce the public to accept in repayment merely another kind of paper and, ideally, to exchange their bullion for paper.† Specifically, Law urged that a central bank be created that by a liberal lending policy would increase the supply of credit.

Law proposed this conception to his native Scotland and to the Kingdom of Savoy, both of whom rejected it. Traveling in Brussels, Vienna, Rome, and elsewhere, he prospered through gambling and speculation. Louis XIV had refused to receive him, but on his death the new Regent became intrigued. Perhaps here was a way out of his problem! In May 1716 Law, by now a French subject, was empowered to open the Banque Générale, headed by himself, on the ground floor of his house on the Place Louis-le-Grand, now the Place Vendôme. The capital was 6 million livres, payable one quarter in cash and three quar-

---

* *The winter of 1709 saw men eating corpses in the streets of Paris.*

† *This was later done in the United States. Under F. D. Roosevelt gold had to be turned in for paper money redeemable in silver; subsequently the bullion backing was repudiated.*

ters in *billets d'état,* government paper that had been selling at 25 percent of face value. By requiring that regional tax payments be in the form of Banque Générale notes, Philippe assured the bank of a steady inflow of funds for its operations, and thus of success. The bank was authorized to issue notes payable on demand in silver coins at their value on the notes' issue date. As they became accepted, Law was able to lower the discount rate from 30 percent to 6 percent and then 4 percent, driving the usurers out of business. The bank, with 6 million livres of capital, soon had 60 million livres of notes outstanding. The French economy surged. Banque Générale notes, since they paid interest and were more convenient, came to sell at a premium over their face value in bullion.

Law soon hatched far grander ideas. He thought he could see a way to induce the French to exchange their gold for paper on an immense scale. France's Louisiana Territory stretched from the Gulf of Mexico to the Rockies in the west and the Great Lakes to the north, including thirteen of our present states. Why not form a company to develop its untapped riches? Of course, settlement in the New World was fearfully arduous. All the sixteenth-century Spanish colonies on the southeastern coast of North America died out; only half the *Mayflower* settlers survived their first winter; and of 750 French pioneers who settled in the Mississippi delta in 1699, four-fifths, often stricken by yellow fever and malaria, perished within one year. (The last act of *Manon Lescaut* quite accurately has Manon and her lover staggering about that sinister landscape waiting to succumb to disease and starvation.) Still, there were enthusiasts. The *Nouveau Mercure* spoke of the Louisiana Territory as "one of the most beautiful and fertile countries in the world," with gold, silver, and emeralds in plenty. The explorer de Remonville gave enthusiastic descriptions. And the government discouraged skeptics: when Cadillac muttered about the difficulties and hazards of establishing a colony, he was hustled off to the Bastille.

Law was granted a charter for a Mississippi development company, the Compagnie de la Louisiane ou d'Occident, which received a twenty-five-year lease on the territory. It was obligated to transplant at least 6,000 French citizens and 3,000 slaves there, and was permitted to raise and maintain its own military force.

He moved fast. The Compagnie obtained a monopoly on growing and selling tobacco—snuff being in wide use at that time. It then integrated upstream, as we would say, by taking over the Senegal Company to assure a supply of slaves for its settlements. After that, it merged with the French East India and China companies, and changed its name to the Compagnie des Indes; it had essentially achieved a monopoly of France's foreign trade. Next it obtained a nine-year monopoly on minting the royal coinage, and finally folded in the Banque Générale, now called the Banque Royale, Law's original creation. This prodigious structure, on paper one of the greatest enterprises in the world, was described proudly by Law as his "System."

But the public had its doubts. Promises are easy! The stock, originally 200,000 shares issued at 500 livres a share, drifted down by late 1718 to a 50 percent discount. Then, in the first four months of 1719, the Banque Royale pumped up the supply of paper notes by 30 percent. Exciting reports about acquisitions, new contracts, and brilliant prospects were propagated. In August the Compagnie acquired the right to act as the national tax collector for nine years. This successfully squashed a rival company, which had been trying to develop an "Anti-System." Law himself, it was revealed, had bought futures contracts in Compagnie des Indes stock at almost twice the market value. The market became intrigued, then excited. The stock recovered to its issue price, doubled, and soon doubled again. The doubters were silenced. Visions of vast, productive Mississippi savannahs, of gold mines, of the fur trade and the tobacco monopoly, of banking profits, added to the wealth of the Orient to be gleaned by the old East India and China companies—all this dazzled the speculators.

Now Law revealed his plan to pay off the national debt. The government would issue 3 percent notes to its creditors. At the same time the Compagnie would issue shares, which the state creditors could buy with the notes. There were few other securities available, and since the shares rose steadily, the noteholders were eager to exchange.

That was how it worked. By August, Compagnie des Indes stock had soared to 5,000 livres a share, ten times its issue price, and by October to 8,000. The state creditors actually had trouble getting as much Compagnie stock as they wanted.

Normally one would expect that so steep a rise would mean that the market would need a rest—a period of consolidation, as the brokers say. Not so. Everyone was cursing themselves for not having bought earlier, and was waiting for a reaction to jump in. Under those conditions there can be no reaction. Also, the succession of new privileges granted to the Compagnie fanned the excitement. Indeed, the real frenzy was just getting under way. Rising prices attracted ever more money, which put prices up further. It was like a waterspout. The Duchesse d'Orléans, the Regent's mother, estimated that more than 300,000 people flooded into Paris from the rest of the country in the hope of getting their hands on some stock in the Compagnie and thus making their fortunes.

The rue Quincampoix, near the Hôtel de Ville, became the focus of intense activity in Compagnie stock: in cafés, in restaurants, out in the street. Men set themselves up as traders, buying and selling to whoever came along, and cleared large daily profits. Cobblers found they could make more money renting out their benches to stock jobbers for up to 200 livres a day, and abandoned their soles and lasts. It was said that a hunchback who pushed his way up and down the teeming street was able to gain a good living by bending over to furnish cramped speculators a space on which to record their transactions. And French society, excited by the speculative fever, gave itself to ostentatious extravagance.

Most of the frantic trading in Compagnie des Indes stock was conducted on the thinnest of margin. Only a 10 percent down payment was required, and even that could be put up in *billets d'état*, which one could buy at a substantial discount. The amount of Banque Royale notes in circulation continued to expand, only one-tenth covered by specie.

Some of the killings that were made by plungers in the space of a few months included a chimney sweep who made 40 million livres and a waiter who made 30 million. A former beggar who got going at the right moment made 70 million, an immense fortune: the entire company had only been capitalized at 100 million at the outset.

Law now found himself the most sought-after man in Europe. Since he could issue new stock below the market, he could enrich anyone at will. Saint-Simon noted in his *Memoirs* that "Law, besieged by applicants and aspirants, saw his door forced, his windows entered from the garden, while some of them came tumbling down the chimney of his office." Law's wife, Catherine Knollys, was in fact still married to her first husband, so his daughter, Marie-Catherine, was illegitimate. Nonetheless, the papal envoy attended her birthday party. "Law is so run after that he has no rest, day or night," wrote the Duchesse d'Orléans. "A duchess kissed his hand before everyone, and if a duchess kisses his hands, what parts of him won't ordinary ladies kiss?"

A Scottish poet, Allen Ramsay, rhapsodized over his compatriot:

The Grateful Gauls your Mem'ry will revere . . .
Who formed them Banks, their sinking Credit rais'd . . .
O More than Man!

Only one thing was lacking: while it's fine to be rich and famous, it's best to have a title, something official. Alas, while Law was now French, he was still a Protestant, during a time when religious controversy was acute. Crusades were launched against Protestants; sometimes they were tortured to force them to abjure their faith. Law found a spiritual adviser, the Abbé Tencin, with whom he had a series of satisfactory meetings, incidentally involving the transfer of several thousand shares of stock. In September 1719, having thus squared the angelic hosts, he was received into the Catholic Church during a gorgeous ceremony in Notre Dame. This cleared the way for his appointment as Controlleur des Finances in January.

In the meanwhile the campaign to induce Frenchmen to move to Mississippi, without which the dream could not be fulfilled, was going badly. Then as now, few wanted to leave *la belle France.* Law had to resort to blue-uniformed press gangs to kidnap unfortunates right off the streets. Judges sentenced thieves, prostitutes, and other undesirables, à la Manon, to deportation to Mississippi. But how many solid merchants or skilled artisans—the men needed to make the settlement function—would agree to spend years of their lives among this dangerous riffraff?

These and other problems finally caused Compagnie des Indes stock to slow its rise. It peaked out near the end of 1719 at the incredible level of 20,000 livres a share, forty times the price it had been issued at not three years earlier. At this figure the market was putting a value on the whole company of over 12 billion livres, compared with a "hard" value of less than 100 million. The profits from the various monopolies could not for many years begin to pay an adequate return at that price. The whole enterprise had become a gigantic bubble waiting to be punctured.

When the times are ripe, the needle is never remote. In January 1720 two courtiers close to the throne, the Prince de Condé and the Prince de Conti, demanded cash for thousands of their shares of Compagnie des Indes stock. To accommodate the princes, Law had to produce whole wagons of gold. Others caught fright and hastened to redeem in turn. So to replace the bullion paid out to meet redemptions, Law had to print rivers of new paper money. Nine presses churned for weeks, producing over 1.5 billion in new paper livres.

In the face of this glut, paper money slipped to a discount as people sought to exchange it for gold. Law made the usual fatal error of trying to control prices by fiat. It was forbidden to possess more than 500 livres in gold or silver, or to make gold or silver plate. Payments of over 100 livres had to be made in paper. Naturally, a black market in coins sprung up at once. When the police came into view, a cry arose, *"Les guets! Les guets!"* ("The cops!") and the contraband vanished. To make French goods more competitive in foreign markets, Law devalued banknotes drastically. Compagnie des Indes stock fell in sympathy, from

9,000 to 5,000. The way speculators think, it matters not that a stock has risen from an issue price of 500 once to 5,000 today; what counts is that it has fallen from an intermediate peak of 20,000. Saint-Simon wrote, "The uproar was general and frightful. Every rich man thought he was ruined; every poor man believed himself reduced to beggary." Law, once fawned upon by royalty, became an object of universal execration. Guards had to protect him from furious mobs trying to break into his house, to injure him whose notice they formerly sought. Violent posters against him appeared on walls around Paris.

Soon he was stripped of his position as Controlleur des Finances; the Regent, once his friend, refused to see him.

But Law was still head of the Compagnie des Indes and the Banque Générale. To hold up his "System" he went back to periodically redeeming Compagnie stock and Banque notes for silver or copper, and then ceremoniously burning the paper. On one such occasion, out of more than fifteen thousand desperate souls who thronged before his door in the hope of exchanging their paper for something tangible, sixteen died of suffocation. But on June 17, 1720, the Banque suspended payments. Commerce slowed and partially shifted to barter. As distribution faltered, there were reports of starvation in some areas.

Law, his life in danger, fled to exile in Holland. His properties in France were seized. Gone, gone the happy days of "Beau" Law, let alone the proud times of "O More Than Man!"

"Last year I was the richest individual who ever lived," he lamented. "Today I have nothing, not even enough to keep alive." After subsisting in various countries, essentially as a gambler, although still proposing great plans to any who would listen, he settled in Venice, and there died, alone, in poverty, and forgotten. France struggled to restore its finances and commerce. Voltaire, ever sardonic, observed, "Paper money has now been restored to its intrinsic value."

THE GREAT WAR LOAN CONVERSION

In 1917, TO FINANCE THE COST OF WORLD WAR I, the British government floated a huge bond issue, the Five Percent War Loan. It was scheduled for repayment thirty years later, in 1947, although it could also be prepaid on three months' notice any time after June 1, 1929.

By 1932, thanks to the Depression, government revenues were low. Just the interest on this single bond issue—of which over £2 billion was outstanding—absorbed 40 percent of all the money collected from income tax. The bonds could not be paid off in cash, so the government decided to persuade the bondholders to accept something else instead.

In late 1931 there was a run on the pound, which slid down from $5 to the $3.25–$3.45 area. Starting the following summer, the Bank of England injected immense amounts of liquidity into the banking system. As a result, interest rates, which reflect the supply of money in relation to the demand for loans, fell to 5 percent in February, 2½ percent in May, and finally 2 percent in June. As yields dropped, investors rushed to nail down the highest returns they could, so the prices of existing bonds soared. Government 2½ percent bonds jumped 10 percent in a week, to

72. The Five Percent War Loan bonds could not rise over 100, though, since the government had the right to pay them off at that price at any time. To increase the impact of this move the government closed off the issue of any new securities, meaning that the market's increased buying power could only be directed to existing issues.

In late June 1932 Chancellor of the Exchequer Neville Chamberlain announced a conversion offer for the entire Five Percent War Loan into a new issue, bearing interest at only 3½ percent, and without any specific maturity. The chancellor exhorted War Loan holders in moving terms to convert to the new issue as a matter of patriotic duty. In case of wavering it was also announced that those who did not refuse the offer would be deemed to have accepted it. And indeed, with the bank rate down at 2 percent thanks to heavy manipulation of the money supply, the 3½ percent coupon looked highly attractive. Since there was no specific maturity date, the owner was also protected forever in his enjoyment of this fine return.

The government created a War Loan Conversion Publicity Bureau, which set off a prodigious barrage of patriotic propaganda to convince the citizenry to accept the deal—like our War Bond appeals in World War II. Every day the Publicity Bureau published a list of institutions that had done their duty.

On July 5 Chancellor Chamberlain called in the heads of the major banks and urged them to give a good example. All agreed except Midland Bank, whose chairman, Reginald McKenna, had himself been Liberal Chancellor of the Exchequer in 1915–1916 and understood Chamberlain's game. The next day McKenna was summoned to the Bank of England, whose governor, Montagu Norman, put him under heavy pressure to convert. McKenna replied that it would not be in the interest of his shareholders. He was correct, but his temerity probably cost him a peerage.* Eventually Midland was persuaded to convert £5 million of the £30 million that it held. The Bank of England

---

* Bernard Baruch flatly refused to lend his name to the War Bond appeals of World War II. War always means inflation, or a debauching of the currency. So whether or not the war is won, the bonds will lose.

itself then agreed to buy out the other £25 million and convert it on its own. So the Publicity Bureau was able to announce—deceptively—that all the clearing banks had converted their holdings.

The hoopla and fanfare surrounding the conversion were intended to bedazzle the small holder. The propaganda was almost too successful. Mounted policemen had to be called out to control the crowds lining up to present their old certificates. Some large holders, however, could see what was happening. John Maynard Keynes, for instance, styled the operation "a bit of a bluff which a fortunate conjunction of circumstances is enabling us to put over on ourselves."

Anyway, thanks to the pressure, the calls to patriotic duty, and the bluff, 92 percent of the holders converted into the new 3½ percent bonds, which by the terms of their issue need never—and doubtless never will—be paid off. Since then, under more usual money market conditions, interest rates have risen and risen and the 3½ percent bonds have declined and declined.

So at the end of the day what happened to the 98 percent of War Loan holders who accepted the conversion?

The calculation is fairly complicated, but in real terms they lost about 99 percent of their money.

Bernie Cornfeld

I.O.S., OR, CORNFELD'S FOLLIES

*We're in the business of totally converting the
proletariat to the leisured class painlessly . . .
it's revolutionary and it's goddam exciting.*
BERNIE CORNFELD

INVESTMENT OVERSEAS SERVICES WAS A DISASTER
for those who trusted it with their savings, but also a tragedy, in
the Aristotelian sense: its protagonist, overreaching himself, was
destroyed by his flaws. But instead of being played out on battle-
fields or in royal castles like the tragedies of the Greek drama-
tists or Shakespeare, it unrolled in company planes and smoky
conference rooms; instead of courtiers and fallen soldiers we encounter slimy lawyers and high-pressure salesmen; instead of a
noble hero overcome by fate we find a collection of hustlers
caught in their own toils. And right on top of the original tragedy came another. I.O.S. was a ghastly double feature.

I. Hubris

Bernie Cornfeld, born in Istanbul in 1927 of Rumanian ancestry, immigrated in 1941 to Brooklyn, where, hindered by a
stammer, he attended public schools. He developed into a fer-
vent socialist. After receiving an M.A. from Columbia's School of
Social Work, he joined a B'nai B'rith program in Philadelphia.
In 1954 he changed tack and became a mutual fund salesman

in New York, moving to Paris in 1955. Selling to the U.S. military such varied items as diamonds and women's underwear, he noticed that there was a large population of marginal Americans floating around Europe: ex-Fulbright scholars, fringe businessmen, writers who didn't actually write. Also, however, hundreds of thousands of G.I.s, collecting steady incomes, stationed with NATO. It occurred to him to put the first category to work selling mutual funds to the second. In New York he had met Jack Dreyfus, late of Mobile, Alabama, founder of a fast-growing mutual fund group. In 1956 Cornfeld got a Dreyfus sales franchise, and within a few years became a major factor in the Dreyfus business, particularly in contractual programs, where the customer undertakes to make regular monthly payments over a period of years. It's a salesman's dream, since the commissions, which are calculated on the amount of the whole contract, not just the early payments, typically eat up all the payments for the first six months.

In those years the market seemed to be a one-way street—up. At first Cornfeld moved around the boulevards and Montmartre bars in rumpled clothes looking like what he was—a runaway socialist social worker. But by 1958 Cornfeld's operation had picked up over seventy salesmen. He adopted a carnival barker manner, dressing in outlandish clothes and hectoring the salesmen with his celebrated line, "Do you sincerely want to be rich?" There were problems with French exchange controls, so the whole setup moved to the rue de Lausanne in Geneva. The stock market, and fund sales, continued to boom. Soon I.O.S. salesmen began turning up all over the world. Then as now, many countries had legal restrictions on the export of capital, and I.O.S.'s Dreyfus Fund sales in due course involved a huge hot-money operation, although nothing compared to what came later.

In late 1960 I.O.S. formed a Luxembourg corporation entitled IIT Fund to invest on a worldwide basis. Investment guidance for IIT was provided by the Bruno A. Hugi Banque Privée, which sounded auspicious but turned out to consist of Dr. Hugi, a retired Union de Banque Suisses director, operating out of his house in a Zurich suburb.

The stock market fell in 1962, and IIT with it: the net asset value per share dropped 22 percent. For an operation based on promises of outstanding performance this was a dismal beginning. Part of the problem was Ed Cowett, a shady lawyer accused of embezzlement from two different legal firms, who was secretary and director of I.O.S. In the frothy market of 1961 Cowett had promoted four companies himself, composed of illiquid "investment letter" stocks in his own name. He then stuffed them into IIT's portfolio at pumped-up prices. All four collapsed. In the resulting stink he was forced off the board but remained as chief counsel, and was restored as a director after only a year in limbo. In time Cornfeld granted vast power within I.O.S. to Cowett, who is usually given credit for the complicated legal arrangements by which I.O.S. escaped taxation, and official control, almost everywhere.

Late in 1962 I.O.S. created the Fund of Funds, a Canadian offshore corporation, which as the name indicated collected a management fee for putting the customers' money into other funds, which themselves also charged management fees.* By a legal device the investors were deprived of any power to vote on the affairs of F.O.F. All authority rested with Cornfeld, Cowett, et al. After a while I.O.S. figured out an improvement on the Fund of Funds idea. Instead of really putting the money into other mutual funds, the Fund of Funds created proprietary "fund accounts" run by outside managers, in which it was the sole investor. Several of these practices were not permitted in the United States, which resulted in I.O.S.'s being forbidden to operate here by the Securities and Exchange Commission. U.S. residents were thus saved the loss of immense sums.

Fund of Funds customers were subjected to an extraordinary pileup of charges: first, a commission on the purchase of F.O.F. shares—and we have seen the salesman's paradise in a mutual

---

* *This seems like an obvious idea, but was novel at the period. I had started a pooled portfolio for clients some time earlier managed by several outside advisers, called the Omnibus Account. There was only one fee and no commissions. My friend Eddie Morgan (son of Richard Whitney's partner mentioned on page 86) tells me of describing this to Cornfeld, whom he encountered in Paris, as "sort of a fund of funds." "A fund of funds, eh?" said Cornfeld, reflectively.*

fund contractual plan. Then, a commission was charged for moving the money into the "fund account," even though this was an internal vehicle. In addition, there was an annual management fee, both for the F.O.F. and the "fund accounts," and a further 10 percent performance fee on all net income and capital gains. Finally, the huge stock exchange commissions generated by all this were not allowed just to slip away.

With all these sources of profit coming out of the hide of the customers, I.O.S. could afford to give its salesmen and other helpers very generous incentives indeed. They got results. Germany, in the middle of its economic miracle, became the prime market. The Fund of Funds reached $100 million within only two years, and went right on growing. IIT eventually reached $900 million, and the entire I.O.S. stable of funds, since others were added on regularly, eventually climbed to $2.5 billion. The top sales managers, running a worldwide force that in time reached 16,000, received shares in the parent company, so that they could hope to become millionaires when it eventually went public.

I.O.S.'s size enabled Cornfeld and Cowett to induce some well-known figures to join the board of directors: James Roosevelt, son of the late president; Sir Eric Wyndham White, former director general of GATT; "Pat" Brown, former governor of California; Erich Mende, head of Germany's Free Democratic party. Roosevelt was helpful in trying to soothe angry governments that cracked down on illegal I.O.S. sales, violations of currency controls, and other such problems. He also impressed the delegates who attended two I.O.S.-sponsored international conventions: Pacem in Terris II, and World Human Rights Law Day, which attracted a number of nations' chief justices, including Earl Warren.

By this time Cornfeld himself was in the full tide of fatal hubris—overweening greed and pride. He even seemed to look physically puffed up. The former socialist and B'nai B'rith worker had two villas in Switzerland, a castle in Haute Savoie, with a moat and a thirteenth-century dining salon (but the most modern of swimming pools), a house in London, an apartment in

Paris, and two in New York. Later came an additional castle in Switzerland. He had a private jet, a Rolls-Royce, a custom-built Lincoln, and other vehicles in case these were inadequate. He was surrounded by pretty girls, and to be sure of a constantly refreshed harem, started model agencies in both New York and Paris. "Where are the *customers'* girls?" John Kenneth Galbraith asked about this *mise en scène,* referring to the Wall Street joke about the visitor who, shown the bankers' flotilla, asks, "Where are the customers' yachts?"

Cornfeld liked to boast about the cosmic merit of selling mutual funds: "We're in the business of totally converting the proletariat to the leisured class painlessly .. . it's revolutionary and it's goddam exciting." "What I have done is apply socialist ideas about redistributing wealth in a free-enterprise context." These ravings did contain an element of truth, except that it was not, alas, poor hopefuls who bought I.O.S.'s wares that were converted to the leisured class, but Cornfeld and Cowett and their henchmen.

The conservative Swiss authorities scarcely liked the tone of all this. They noticed that of more than a thousand I.O.S. headquarters employees in Geneva only eighty-seven had work permits. All but those eighty-seven were expelled and I.O.S. was hit with a million-franc fine. A new headquarters was hastily thrown together just over the French border.

At its peak in the late 1960s, I.O.S. had sixteen funds, five insurance companies, and a stable of banks, real estate companies, and other odds and ends. However, its investment methods were becoming increasingly shaky. The Fund of Funds, running an internal performance race, hired a stable of hot-stock gunslingers who chased each other out on thinner and thinner ice, buying stocks in flimsy conglomerates and "concept" companies, hoping to scalp a few points before they fell apart. They manufactured performance by subscribing to unregistered "letter" stock, sold by doubtful companies at big discounts from the listed market. One could then show a price closer to market for appraisal purposes, and look clever for a while. As Fred Alger, one of the Fund of Funds managers, put it, "We bought stocks at $90, not because they were worth $90, but because we believed that tomorrow they would be at $120. When we went home nights, we just hoped the goddammed company would still be there the next morning." Sometimes they were and sometimes they weren't.

Then I.O.S. began buying securities issues for its funds that had been packaged and marked up by some of its own subsidiaries, thus in effect using its customers' money to generate underwriting commissions for itself, in addition to all the other commissions.

The most notorious irregularity involved Fund of Funds' transaction with King Resources, a company that sold tax-oriented oil-drilling deals, headed by John King, a flamboyant Denver tycoon. Cornfeld was desperate to show good performance for Fund of Funds. He wanted to have a public issue of I.O.S. stock, so that he and his key associates could cash in. To do that, F.O.F. sales had to continue strong. That required a record that the salesmen could sell: F.O.F. had to keep going up. But the market had declined all through 1969. What to do? Cornfeld thought he saw a way to manufacture performance. He would put a big wad of Fund of Funds money into speculative oil property that had no quoted market value. Then he could claim that the real value was whatever he said it was. Of course, this violated the essence of the Fund of Funds idea: funds are suppose to invest in liquid, readily marketable assets. Too bad! So the Fund established a Natural Resources Account, which King managed, often himself selling his own oil properties to it, suitably marked up.

The Account paid King $11 million for a half-interest in drilling rights on 22 million acres in the Swerdrup Basin in the Canadian Arctic. Four-fifths of the acreage consisted of ice-covered seas, the most inauspicious possible place for drilling. No matter! Fund of Funds then sold a tenth of this interest, at a much higher price, in large part right back to King himself, and on easy installment terms. Little or no cash changed hands. This cozy transaction was taken as establishing a new value of $156 million for the acreage just bought for $11 million. That amount was "prudently" cut back to a trifling $102 million, just in time to give a huge kick to the Fund of Funds' year-end value, thanks to which I.O.S. dealt itself a 1969 year-end "performance fee" of almost $10 million.

To dress things up for the I.O.S. public stock offering, IIT also did its share of hanky-panky. The fund had been started in 1960 at $5 a share, which dropped $3.53 in 1962, before recovering to $8.82 in 1969. So to improve appearances the I.O.S. prospectus claimed that IIT had only come under I.O.S.'s management in 1962, at the bottom, not 1960, and showed the performance calculations from the later date.

Finally came the great, long-awaited moment of the public offering. In September 1969 I.O.S., from Canada, offered 11 million shares to the public at $10, or $110 million in all. The insiders, about 500 of them, were going to get their hands on some capital at last. The lead underwriters included Drexel, Harriman, Ripley; Smith, Barney; and Banque Rothschild, Paris. The offering was successful and the stock advanced over its issue price.

By December it had sagged off again to 11½. The insiders were concerned: the issue *had* to go up. Cowett, now president, had I.O.S. secretly transfer millions of dollars to himself and John King to buy stock. I.O.S. also advanced funds to its own stock-option plan to acquire stock that the insiders were selling. To heat up the market about $35 million was laid out.

It had been predicted that I.O.S. would show a $25 million profit for 1969; also, that it would sell $4.5 billion of funds in 1970, on top of the $2 billion already under management, which Cornfeld proclaimed would reach $15 billion by 1975.

After making this prediction he flew to Acapulco aboard Playboy Club president Hugh Hefner's black DC-9—called *Black Bunny*—together with a clutch of girl groupies, attendants, and boosters. CBS, it was learned, was to do a TV film on his successes. This was Cornfeld's apogee.

II. Nemesis

Just beneath the surface things were decomposing. In the first place, the costs, commissions, and leaks were so extensive that

I.O.S. wasn't really making money at its regular business of running mutual funds. Rather, the profits came increasingly from a succession of special deals, which could scarcely be predicted. By February 1970 the staff had cut their estimate of 1969 earnings from $25 million to $17.9 million. By May 1970, with a bear market depressing both stock prices and fund sales, a $7 to $13 million *loss* was predicted for the first six months of the year. Horrors! Fund redemptions started to pick up as the shareholders began to realize that the situation was like musical chairs: the last one out would get stuck with a slop chest of illiquid and overvalued assets. Soon redemptions reached $25 million a week. The three largest funds, F.O.F., IIT, and Venture Fund International, were to lose half their assets in a matter of months. The manager of the Banque Rothschild, which had joined its name to Cornfeld's and Cowett's a few months previously by underwriting the public issue, now declared that I.O.S. was cooked. The stock collapsed to less than half its issue price, signaling to the whole world that things were rotten and terrifying both its own shareholders and the investors in its funds—often the same people. Reports started to fly that I.O.S. was running out of cash. The company issued a reassuring—but false—statement that all was well.

The directors realized that everything was coming unstuck right in their hands. Cornfeld, exposed and discredited, was replaced by Sir Eric Wyndham White as chairman.

Cornfeld was finished, his claims about "worldwide people's capitalism" exposed as hypocritical cant, his showy boards of directors and public convocations revealed as camouflage for abuse of trust. The tragedy was played out; the curtain had fallen.*

Great American Management and Research, founded in 1967 by Keith Barish, a five-foot-six twenty-two-year-old Miamian, had a career curiously parallel to I.O.S.. It was a fund to invest in real estate. Funds are supposed to be liquid while real estate is not, so to escape the S.E.C. Barish, like Cornfeld, took his operation offshore to Panama, Curacao, and such havens. I.O.S. had hired James Roosevelt and Donald Nixon, so Barish collected Kennedy alumni: two Kennedy ambassadors, a Cabinet undersecretary and an assistant secretary, two Kennedy staffers, and as the plum in the pudding, Pierre Salinger, J.F.K.'s sometime press secre-

III. Catastrophe

Alas, there was a sequel, even grimmer than what had gone before.

The Directors of I.O.S. needed a savior to restore confidence, one with enough financial strength to hold things together until the hemorrhage of fund redemptions could be stanched. John King and Banque Rothschild both put themselves forward, but their claims were set aside in favor of an unknown who looked respectable and was introduced by managing director Karlweiss of the Banque Privée de Genève, an Edmond de Rothschild company. He was Robert Vesco, a minor American industrialist, who loved the idea of moving on equal terms with the business elite of the world, of being accepted as a financial aristocrat. A Cornfeld assistant announced breathlessly, after a few minutes' meeting, that he had been "in the presence of one of the greatest financial geniuses of the twentieth century." This important news was supposed to rally the fleeing troops. They should have fled even faster.

Vesco's company, International Controls, formerly Cryogenics, Inc., was having its own troubles. Vesco thought he saw how to shore things up.* To get his foot in the door, he offered

---

tary, to be titular head of the sales force. Six hundred salesmen worldwide collected $200 million for Gramco by late 1969. In addition to management fees, the company extracted a commission of 5 percent of the gross value of assets bought, which was often many times the cash invested, since the properties were acquired with mortgages. Like I.O.S., Gramco went public in 1969, also, like I.O.S., at $10 a share. It advanced to a peak of 38, giving Barish and the New Frontiersmen ample opportunity to bail out. Within a year it had halted redemptions and fallen to $1.50. Barish hired three bodyguards and became a heavy backer of McGovern for president.

* Once, flying back from Geneva to New York in a Swissair 747 in that curious dome above the front of the plane, I recognized Vesco, who was frequently in the papers during this period, sitting cross-legged sideways on a sofa in the rear of the compartment. Spread in front of him was a large chart, which he studied hour after hour, most of the way across the Atlantic. At the time I presumed it was a flow chart of a factory, but now I suppose it must have been a diagram his staff had prepared of I.O.S. and that he was already figuring out how to plunder it.

I.O.S. a loan of $5 million. He got the money from Butlers Bank, a tiny affair in Nassau, Bahamas. (Alan Butler was married to Shirley Oakes, daughter of the Sir Harry Oakes who had been bludgeoned and set afire in his bed in Nassau's most bizarre murder mystery.) As soon as Vesco received the $5 million, he had I.O.S. put the same amount back in the bank.

Through a chain of dummy companies he then contracted to buy Cornfeld's own I.O.S. stock for $5.5 million. To raise the cash, he had Arthur Lipper Corp., a brokerage firm that did a vast amount of I.O.S. business, put $5.5 million into Butlers Bank, which loaned the money for the closing. In other words, Vesco essentially financed his purchase of I.O.S. by using I.O.S.'s own money and brokerage largesse.

After signing the contract selling his stock, Cornfeld and a nestful of girlies disappeared in a jet to Cuernavaca, Mexico. Later he made the mistake of returning to Geneva and was immediately jailed, to be released, in spite of his lawyers' diligent efforts, only after almost a year. He was eventually acquitted of the specific charges, which related to Switzerland.

Most of the I.O.S. big-name directors soon quit, but James Roosevelt switched his allegiance to Vesco, who also hired Donald Nixon, nephew of another president, and indeed was later charged with giving Nixon an illegal campaign contribution.

The looting spree now moved into high gear. Here are a few examples. Forty percent of I.O.S.'s European and Bahamian banking assets, worth some $5 million, were exchanged for shares in a "bank" belonging to Vesco crony Friederich Weymer, formerly of Butlers Bank. Weymer had bought his "bank" from Butlers for a mere $300,000 in cash plus $1.5 million in notes. Weymer became head of the old I.O.S. European and Bahamian banking operations.

Vesco then had I.O.S. repay International Controls the $5 million it had borrowed to start the whole transaction, and issue 6 million shares (worth $60 million at the price of public issue of two years before) as a "bonus."

In a series of complicated maneuvers another Vesco associate was permitted to acquire a controlling interest in assets valued three years before at $100 million for a cash outlay of $2,000.

Sixty million dollars of Fund of Funds money was invested in a private Vesco vehicle, Interamerican Capital, in Costa Rica. Vesco hoped to get permission to live there, so among its principals were a number of influential Costa Ricans.

The different operations are too complicated to set out in detail, but according to the S.E.C. some $250 million was extracted from several I.O.S. funds; others have put it at $1 billion.

For a time Vesco lived in Nassau, protected by bodyguards. Expelled, he moved into a fortified compound in Costa Rica. When he was expelled from Costa Rica he went to Nicaragua. NBC reported that he was behind an international narcotics operation. In November 1983 federal prosecutors accused him of masterminding a smuggling plot from his latest residence, Cuba, and in 1984 of being involved in illegal transfers of U.S. technology to the Soviet Union.

The S.E.C. has been trying for all these years to extradite him for trial, unsuccessfully. The Cubans seem most unlikely to cooperate.

One of Cornfeld's Geneva lawyers, Pierre Sciclounoff, in addition to his successful legal practice has become a representative of Bulgarian interests: a leader of Bulgarian-Swiss friendship societies, cultural exchanges, and the like.

John King was sentenced to jail for his part in these matters; Ed Cowett died on his way to testify at that trial.

Cornfeld has been living in California. He used to talk of large real estate projects and important movie productions. A while back he was convicted of making phone calls with a "blue box" to avoid paying tolls. The telephone company caught him anyway. Now balding, pudgy, and sporting a full beard, he has announced a venture to produce sexually invigorating diet products.

THE FRENCH REVOLUTIONARY
HYPERINFLATION

*

THE IDEA OF DEBAUCHING THE CURRENCY AS A short road to prosperity seems to recur in a country as soon as its leaders have had long enough to forget what happened the last time.

By 1789 France was once again in financial straits, because of military costs, royal extravagance, and the chaos that came with the Revolution. Gold and silver currency was disappearing from circulation, as the public hoarded it, in fear of some new catastrophe. The wild speculation, corruption, and economic collapse that had followed John Law's introduction of paper money was generally remembered, but not in its full misery. So once again it seemed tempting to prime the pump and get the government some cash, by reintroducing paper money to increase the currency supply.

Some members of the Assemblée feared the consequences of issuing paper money. Mirabeau, its most influential member, denounced it as "a loan to an armed robber" and argued for the abolition of even the term "paper money" itself. Eventually, though, he went along with the majority, who felt that it could be attempted safely for two reasons: first, the new constitutional government would be less corruptible than the old royal one had been, and so would be more prudent in the use of this dangerous weapon. Second, the Revolution had expropriated the immense estates of the Church, amounting to over a quarter of all French property, and it was proposed that any new issue of paper money should be secured by these lands. In order to prevent the issue from competing with the existing specie currency, notes would be issued only in large denominations: 200, 300, and 1,000 livres. (A livre corresponded roughly to an unskilled worker's daily wage. A skilled worker earned not quite twice that.)

After passionate discussion the Assemblée finally decreed the issuance of 400 million livres' worth of *assignats*—government notes secured by the estates of the Church. They bore a 3 percent interest rate which, it was hoped, would make them attractive enough to coax specie back out of hiding.

The revolutionary government had the *assignats* impressively engraved. Patriotic slogans and devices twined their way around a pudgy silhouette of Louis XVI, looking sometimes to the left and sometimes to the right. He was still king, although much of his power had passed to the Assemblée. The daily interest was printed in the margin: a 1,000-livre note earned the bearer, daily, 20 deniers. Each note was embossed and signed. The king, as usual in these affairs, lent his high patronage to the scheme. An otherwise obscure Monsieur Sarot was widely commended for having sold his house entirely for *assignats*.

Under the impact of this stimulus business did pick up. Unfortunately the government, as always, instantly found a thousand uses for its financial windfall, and within only five months was back clamoring for more. Some members of the Assemblée, including Talleyrand and Necker (who was finance minister intermittently through the period), foresaw the seeds of real trouble and objected vehemently. Brillat-Savarin predicted that any new issue would decline sharply in value. But finally, by a close vote, in September 1789 the Assemblée decreed the issue of another 800 million livres, this time in noninterest-bearing notes. It was solemnly specified that the total of notes in circulation must never, never exceed 1.2 billion livres.

Alas, easy money is addictive. Only nine months after this

issue a new one was voted, of 600 million livres, and in December 1791 another, of 300 million. The following April came another, of 300 million, making a total of 2.4 billion in circulation.

As the torrent of paper poured out of the presses, specie vanished, goods were hoarded, and prices flew upward. Speculators bought with borrowed funds whatever was available, intending to repay in the future with depreciated currency. Workers and peasants with fixed wages began to suffer acutely as prices rose. Early in 1793 a desperate mob plundered two hundred stores in Paris.

The government attempted the usual measures, starting with a series of forced loans to soak up excess liquidity. Louis XVI and Marie Antoinette were beheaded and the king's head was also removed from the *assignats*, but the total volume in circulation reached 4.2 billion. Price controls were instituted, under the so-called Law of the Maximum.

In response, as always, farmers and manufacturers decreased their output. As a result many towns had to initiate rationing. The government, to force acceptance of its paper money, decreed twenty years' imprisonment in chains for anyone selling its notes at a discount: then it was made punishable by death to differentiate between paper and specie in setting the price of a transaction, or to invest abroad. Nothing worked.

In 1794, the year Robespierre was himself guillotined as the Revolution, inevitably, devoured its own children, *assignats* in circulation reached 7 billion; by May 1795, 10 billion; two months later, 14 billion—a thousand times over the 1.2 million limit set four years earlier.

Prices soared correspondingly, but not wages. Speculators who had bought with borrowed money prospered; old-fashioned savers were reduced to penury. Morals, patriotism, and thrift gave way to the extravagant ostentation of the newly rich. Gambling and speculation replaced productive investment.*

---

* We are, of course, witnessing the same phenomenon today in many countries, including America. Within my own memory inflation has increased most prices by ten to twenty times. The agreeable nickel subway or bus ride of my youth now costs 90¢. The class of serious, frugal small

The Directorate attempted a new device. The plates used to print the *assignats,* of which 40 billion were now in circulation, were carted to the Place Vendôme, smashed, and burned, after which a new paper currency, the *mandats,* were issued, again backed by expropriated land. Merely expressing skepticism about the *mandats'* value was made punishable by fine, and a second offense by four years in chains. Fines and imprisonment were decreed for those unwilling to accept *mandats* as payment. Still, it took only a few months for them to lose 97 percent of their value. The plates and printing equipment for the *mandats* were in turn publicly broken up. By this time, a gold coin had increased six hundred times in nominal value compared to paper.

Finally, in 1797, all *assignats* and *mandats* were repudiated, and became essentially worthless.

At Bonaparte's first cabinet meeting after he became consul he was asked what was to be done. "I will pay cash or pay nothing," he replied. And so he did. He never went back to paper money.

---

savers, their capital wiped out (sometimes by rent control: see Afterword), hesitates to build for the future and prefers to spend today; since long-term safe investment has become almost impossible, it is replaced by speculation and gambling in commodities. One hopes that good sense is slowly returning, but usually it takes a great shock to do it.

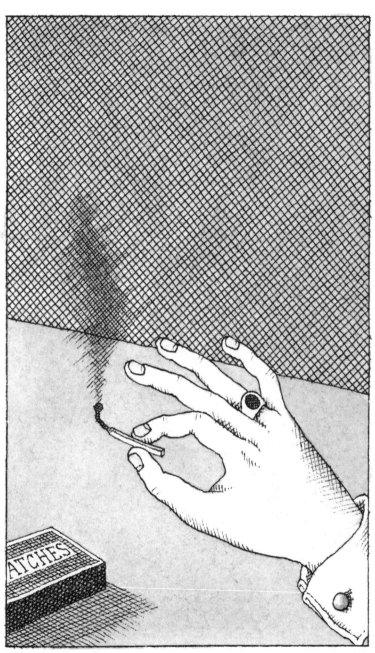

Ivar Krueger, the Swedish Match King

IVAR KRUEGER, THE SWEDISH
MATCH KING

Unlikely as it seems, there was a period in the mid-1920s when a single man made two-thirds of all the matches in the world; that is, he controlled the two hundred-odd factories that made them, in some thirty-five countries. He held a legally enforced monopoly in fifteen countries, a de facto monopoly in nine others, and dominated the market in at least ten more.

In the Middle Ages and thereafter European rulers often raised money by selling monopoly rights to certain manufactures or mercantile activities; even into our own time many governments maintain state monopolies on tobacco; matches and tobacco go hand in hand, of course. These monopolies require careful policing, including undercover operations. In the heyday of the Krueger dominance, Peru fielded armies of *agents provocateurs* who would pester prosperous-looking individuals on the streets of Lima, preferably foreigners, for a light. If the victim produced a non-monopoly match, or even a cigarette lighter, he was liable for a stiff fine—several thousand dollars in our money—of which half went to the informant: no small sum in Peru in those days.

But how did Ivar Krueger ever reach this extraordinary position? In the first place, making matches was as characteristic an industry in timber-covered Sweden as winemaking in France. The principle of the safety match had been developed in Sweden, and by the late nineteenth century there was a proliferation of match factories. Krueger's father ran three of them. Exports almost tripled from 1870 to 1900, and had doubled again by World War I.

As a child Ivar Krueger manifested three of the traits for which he later became celebrated: memory for detail, zeal in concocting nefarious designs, and megalomania. He could recite sermons almost verbatim after returning from church; he would steal examination questions from his school principal's office and retail them to his classmates; and once, passing the Royal Palace, he announced, "I'm going to have one like it one day."

After receiving a university degree in engineering, young Krueger in 1899 took ship to America, and then set forth on a voyage of several years to Cuba and Mexico, working as a construction engineer. He was one of eleven engineers on a bridge project near Vera Cruz, Mexico; all but two died of yellow fever. Once more in the United States, he was employed by various firms, notably the George A. Fuller Construction Company, and then went to South Africa to work on the Carlton Hotel in Johannesburg.

Returning to Sweden in 1907, he started his own construction firm, Krueger & Toll, said to be the first in Sweden to guarantee customers against either delays or cost overruns. They received a number of major commissions, including the Stockholm City Hall—the *Stadhus*—and the Olympic Stadium. In time it spread into other European countries and diversified into banking and films. Greta Garbo's first screen appearance was in a Krueger-backed production. The next move was back into matches. By 1915 ten companies had been assembled under his banner as United Swedish Match Factories. World War I interrupted Sweden's supply of phosphorus and potash; by securing better sources, Krueger was able to outmaneuver and overcome his chief competitor, Jönköping-Vulcan; the two enterprises were merged as Svenska Tändsticks A.B.—the Swedish Match Company.

Sure enough, Sweden's leading architect was commissioned to build a splendid edifice of marble and bronze to house the new company . . . not far from the Royal Palace. Krueger had achieved one of his ambitions. The citizens of Stockholm soon began calling it the Match Palace. Krueger himself, inevitably, became known as the Match King (Tändsticks Küngen).

His own office in the Palace was notable for its Gobelins tapestries, wood-paneled walls, and fine antiques. A smaller, soundproofed, completely private office had a red light over the door: when it was lit, the King could not be disturbed for any reason whatever. He was thinking. Reverently known as the Silence Room, it contained sleeping and washing facilities. Krueger occasionally spent the night there.

Krueger's conquest of the world match market proceeded forcefully, often by guile. Belgium was conquered by having a certain Sven Huldt prevail upon a number of other producers to group together under him in order to gain the strength to resist Krueger. That objective achieved, Huldt promptly sold out to Swedish Match. Krueger was more than willing to buy the services of agents of influence to persuade his victims to yield gracefully.

But what about the countries with government match monopolies? Governments get themselves into financial straits, and someone with cash can be confident of his welcome. Krueger would arrange for a loan to a needy country, tied to his taking over the national match monopoly. Turkey, Yugoslavia, Guatemala, Equador, and Peru were penetrated in this way. Millions went to Latvia and Estonia, to Rumania, Hungary, and Greece. For lending 75 million francs to France, he received the country's highest decoration. A newspaper editorial pronounced him "Olympian."

By this time the Match King was one of the most famous figures on the international business scene. In addition to Stockholm, he had residences in Paris and New York. He arranged for Lee, Higginson, a small but eminent Boston firm, investment bankers for General Motors and AT&T, to underwrite an initial securities offering of $21.8 million in stock and $15 million in debentures for his American company, International Match Corporation. Eventually Krueger raised a total of $145 million in the United States. On the way over on the *Berengaria* to close the Lee, Higginson deal, Krueger created something of a stir by booking the ship's commercial radio transmitter and receiver exclusively, around the clock, for the entire voyage, so that nobody else could send or receive messages. When the vessel docked, one of the reporters meeting it asked Krueger if he had a light. Rather than pulling out the box he always carried, the Match King, smiling faintly, replied, "Sorry, gentlemen, I never seem to have one with me." The reporters ate it up.

This low-key manner was typical of Krueger. He was a modest, pale, formal man, never flamboyant or domineering. On one occasion he arrived for a gay garden party on Long Island dressed entirely in black, complete with black bowler hat, like an undertaker. He even marched onto the court in this lugubrious outfit and played tennis!

In the heady days of the late 1920s, with stocks hitting new highs every day, Krueger appeared to have an infallible golden touch. But in fact he was doing some perilous things. One of his favorite devices was an extensive use of off-the-books conduits. Roughly four hundred were formed, often based in Liechtenstein and other jurisdictions with minimal controls, and funds were whirled around among them in a way that only Krueger himself could keep straight. Even though the directors of Krueger's corporations were generally puppets, the conduit companies' transactions were not reported to them or to the parent company's auditors. Even Krueger's personal assistant, Kristor Littorin, knew "no more than the lift boy at the Match Palace," in the words of a later investigator. The Match King wanted no prime minister, no privy council. An admirer of Napoleon, who held no councils of war, he liked to quote an observation of the emperor that "one first-class brain is enough for an army." International Match paid an absolutely regular 11 percent cash dividend; the world was inclined to take the rest on faith. This permitted Krueger to funnel $16 million of the first Lee, Higginson underwriting, for instance, not directly into the match business but to Continental Investment Corporation of Vaduz, 80 percent of whose capitalization consisted of Krueger's "personal guarantee." Why this arrangement? If anyone asked, Krueger would calmly recite facts, names, and figures until the questioner was overwhelmed—but never give it in writing. Sometimes he would link a stock issue with a rumored new monopoly, to be secured by a loan to the host country. In 1924, for instance, he told his board that Spain had agreed to pay 16 percent interest on a loan of 124 million pesetas—more than enough to cover the 11 percent dividend and make a handsome profit. But the only other person who saw the actual loan agreement thought it seemed fake: the date was a curiously casual "January 1925." In July there was a similarly dubious loan to Poland.

In the great crash of 1929 and the early 1930s, the Match King seemed to repose serenely on a financial rock. Just two days after Black Thursday, Krueger signed an agreement to lend $125 million to Germany. "Securities in companies like International Match which operate on sound foundations will always be good," he intoned. President Herbert Hoover received him regularly at the White House to discuss the economic situation and what to do about it.

But back in Boston they weren't quite so sure. Lee, Higginson sent Donald Durant, who looked after the International Match account, to Stockholm to sniff around. Krueger gave his usual prodigious recitation of financial and industrial data, and to clinch matters held a splendid ball, attended by the flower of the nobility and the diplomatic corps; or so it seemed. It later emerged that many of the guests were hired for the occasion. An eminent International Match director, Percy Rockefeller, came to see for himself. His seance with the King in the Match Palace impressed him hugely. Krueger's telephone rang at various times during their talk. Krueger would say, "I am always available to talk to Mr. Baldwin. Good morning, Prime Minister! How good of you to telephone." Calls were put through from

Premier Poincaré of France and, of all people, Joseph Stalin. Mr. Rockefeller, scarcely a neophyte, since he was on sixty other boards, was agog. "He is on the most intimate terms with the heads of European governments," he reported back to his awed fellow directors. "Gentlemen, we are fortunate indeed to be associated with Ivar Krueger." Alas, later investigations revealed that these cozy dialogues were just stage business conducted via a dummy telephone.

In 1931 Krueger attracted notice by *over*paying his U.S. taxes by $150,000 . . . cheaper and more convincing than a conventional advertising campaign to assert his solvency. But as the Depression deepened, the wonderful structure began to come unstuck. Even matches, solid, basic business that they are, made less money, and of course Krueger had to come up with huge amounts of cash, not only for the famous 11 percent dividend but for the loans to governments that were the basis of his monopolies. With the stock and bond markets collapsing, the money had to come from banks, and the banks were feeling sick themselves. Krueger was reduced to desperate expedients, borrowing several times on the same security, even faking the collateral. He would give a bank manager a stack of banknotes and request a deposit receipt for, say, 100 million francs. If, when finally counted later in the day, the amount proved to be much less, Krueger would apologize for the confusion and accept a receipt for the smaller amount, but in the interim the 100 million franc receipt would have done its work in another quarter. One of his most outrageous frauds was personally forging $143 million in Italian obligations. The job was so slapdash that the same signature—that of Director of Finances Giovanni Boselli—was rendered in several different styles.

The noose tightened. With the banks running dry and skepticism growing it became ever harder for the once omnipotent Match King to raise the immense sums required to keep the machine going as earlier creditors had to be paid off. A relatively small problem finally did it. Krueger owned an interest in L.M. Ericsson, a leading Swedish telephone equipment company; ITT had expressed interest in buying his holdings for $11 million. Then ITT backed out. Something snapped. *"Jag minus inte längre, jag blir galen,"* groaned the failing King: "I can't think anymore; I'm going crazy." He had a small stroke, became vague and listless. Since there was nobody else who understood his fantastic construction well enough to prop it up, it had to fall with its master. On March 12, 1932, Krueger shot himself. A Price, Waterhouse audit revealed that both Krueger & Toll and International Match were bankrupt.* Claims against the Match King's estate eventually passed $1 billion.

---

* *Among the many sad consequences of the Match King's overthrow I might cite one, the strange end of St. Phalle & Co., members of the New York Stock Exchange. Heavy losses caused the firm to send the youngest St. Phalle brother, Claude, who told me the story, to Europe in a desperate search for an investor to shore up their firm. Coming back empty-handed, he met on the boat a European financier who was seeking just such an opportunity. They did the deal. Since the exchange did not permit for-eign-controlled firms, the European joined as a limited partner of each St. Phalle brother individually. He sought the association because he needed a mechanism for supporting his securities in the New York market.*

The man was none other than Ivar Krueger, the securities he wanted to have supported were Krueger & Toll bonds, and his investment in St. Phalle & Co. was in the form of more of those bonds. When Krueger & Toll collapsed, St. Phalle & Co. sank for the last time.

Ferdinand de Lesseps in Panama

THE FRENCH PANAMA CANAL COMPANY

F ERDINAND DE LESSEPS ENTERED THE FRENCH
Foreign Service at nineteen. In 1833, at the age of twenty-seven,
he was posted to Cairo. Perhaps because he was unencumbered
by either an engineering or financial background, he there conceived the idea of reviving the ancient project of opening a
water link between the Mediterranean and the Red Sea. Sea-
borne commerce between Europe and Asia could thus avoid the
long, dangerous voyage around Africa.

Decades of studies and negotiations followed, while de Lesseps held diplomatic assignments in a number of countries. Relieved of his post as Minister of France at Madrid, he turned all
his energies to the project. In 1854 he received a concession
from the Khedive to pierce the canal and in 1858 formed a company for this purpose. Just over half the money was put up by
French investors and about 44 percent by the Khedive. Work
began in 1859.

In 1868 the Suez Canal was finally opened, amidst vast international excitement, by the Empress Eugénie in person, supported by a brilliant assemblage of notables.

For months there were too few hours in the day for all the international banquets, *vins d'honneur*, decorations, ceremonies,

and investitures; only God can have heard more eulogies. De Lesseps' prestige—and self-confidence—rose with every newspaper headline, every procession, every flowery toast. The impression of his omnipotence was confirmed when the hero, sixty-four, took to wife a girl forty-four years his junior. The happy pair was to beget twelve children, the procession only slowing when he reached eighty.* The only problem was to identify a prodigious new achievement to crown his career. In due course a worthy project was found: cutting a passage across Central America, to spare mariners crossing from the Atlantic and Pacific oceans the difficult voyage down the whole coast of South America, around fierce Cape Horn, graveyard of ships, and then all the way up the other coast.

In 1878, representatives of twenty-two interested countries were invited to Paris to consider the best solution. Less than a third of the 138 delegates were engineers. The U.S. delegation favored the comparatively inexpensive approach of building dams and locks on the San Juan River, from the Atlantic up to Lake Nicaragua, then down again to the Pacific with a canal and more locks. Unfortunately a French promoter, Napoleon Bonaparte Wyse, had, after a brief survey, extracted a concession from Colombia to build a sea-level canal across the Isthmus of Panama along the course of the Chagres River. The concession could be made available at a price. This convenient—and French—solution appealed to de Lesseps, who pushed irresistibly for the Panama approach, in spite of many objections on grounds of technical difficulty and huge expense. Bunau-Varilla, his chief assistant, has described the air of courteous incomprehension that settled over him when detailed problems were raised. His faith and self-confidence were unshaken by facts.

Finally the matter came to a vote. The French delegation, at a moment when only half the group was on hand, yielded to de Lesseps' pressure and chose Panama. Of the full 138 delegates, 78, a majority French, voted for Panama, but, ominously, none

* When de Lesseps first saw Princess Mathilde Bonaparte, a mid-century beauty noted for her vast décolletages, he turned to Dumas fils and whispered rapturously, "Ah! If only she were an isthmus!"

of the 5 delegates from the French Society of Engineers. Not one delegate had actually been to Central America!* The cost of the project was estimated at 530 million to 1.2 billion francs, and the time for its realization eight to twelve years. De Lesseps was, of course, first obliged to take care of Monsieur Napoleon Bonaparte Wyse, who held the concession and in view of the international significance of the project consented to hand over his concession for a quick profit of only 3,000 percent. There was another problem: an American railroad company operated along the route. Its line was bought out at a price of 125 million francs, representing a relatively restrained profit of only 300 percent.

Now the problem was to raise the money. De Lesseps was sure that his prestige would enable him to charm it out of the ground. He set off on a road show around France, bypassing the bankers who had hoped to get the job. He also neglected to pay off the newspaper publishers and journalists, whose enthusiasm was linked to their subsidies. As a result, sinister rumors began to circulate: Panama was so ridden by deadly diseases that Europeans could not survive there, the route was impracticable, the budget inadequate. And de Lesseps was seventy-four years old.

Troubled, the provincial investors kept their hands in their pockets. The issue was a failure. With less than 10 percent of the stock issue subscribed, the money had to be returned.

It was time to whip up some excitement. De Lesseps embarked for Panama in person. To prove that the problem of disease was not as grave as believed he brought along his young wife and three of their children. They remained a month, and indeed nobody was stricken by fever. The weather was agreeable; there were no problems. The old lion and his young family returned to France amidst general acclamation. Faith was restored . . . helped this time by massive subsidies to the newspapers.

---

* *Adolphe Godin de Lepinay, one of the French engineers, realized that the plans for a sea-level canal were impractical and put forward an alternative plan for a lock canal. He sat down to a "cacophony of booing." This plan was later adopted by the United States.*

The second attempt at a stock flotation succeeded splendidly. Set at a modest figure, 300 million francs, it was 100 percent oversubscribed by 100,000 eager investors. Unfortunately, the excess subscriptions, which would have been invaluable later on, had to be refused.

In 1881 digging began. Right from the start frightful problems arose. Alas, it was all too true about the danger of disease: de Lesseps' visit had been in the dry season, but with the rains came clouds of insects. The huge holes in the earth created by the excavations soon filled up into stagnant pools, ideal breeding grounds for mosquitoes, which only later were discovered to transmit both yellow fever and malaria. Workers and supervisors fell side by side: the death toll reached the tens of thousands (50,000 by some accounts), including two-thirds of all the Frenchmen who set foot on the Isthmus.*

The engineering problems were indescribable. The earth, manageable in the dry season, turned into horrible quagmires of mud with the onset of the rains. Enormous masses of excavated earth continually slid back into the cuts, carrying with them equipment, rails, and even buildings. The Chagres could rise more than twenty feet in forty-eight hours and turn into a furious torrent.† Furthermore, far from de Lesseps' amiable dream of a canal without locks, the proposed route turned out to be barred by the Culebra ("cobra") formation, at its peak 330 feet above sea level.

The work, originally placed under one outside contractor, was taken over by the company itself. That system also failed. De Lesseps tried farming the job out to six outside contractors. Nothing worked. Waste and confusion reigned. The cost of food and lodging in the region quintupled, and moral standards collapsed. It was said that the only activities that flourished were gambling, prostitution, and coffin-making.

The hopelessness of the sea-level plan was finally accepted, and in 1885 a lock canal was decided on after all. But funds were

---

* *Compare Ivar Krueger's experience in Vera Cruz, page 62.*

† *As one of the canal chaplains said of the Chagres: "they must dam it, or it will damn them."*

running low. Like an exhausted horse, the public could only barely be flogged into putting up more millions. The following year de Lesseps, hoping to shore things up, paid a second visit to Panama. Still living in the world of his vast dreams and conceptions, he may not have understood the irretrievability of the disaster. His son Charles assumed day-to-day control, as his family sheltered him from adverse reports.

One financing technique that retained a measure of popularity was the combination bond issue and lottery. However, it required approval by the French Chamber of Deputies and Senate. Legions of these dignitaries discovered that only cash could reconcile their consciences to the suppression of the information they now had on actual conditions. Even several ministers felt they needed similar encouragement. A pair of noted swindlers, Cornelius Herz and Baron Jacques de Reinach, were among the most energetic dispensers of this largesse. And of course the newspapers, troubled by their earlier role in the promotion of this affair, required massive subsidies to overcome their urge to reveal what they knew.

In 1889, the crumbling edifice could no longer be supported by any amount of official bribes and paid newspaper accounts. After ten years and 400 million francs the Compagnie Internationale et Universelle du Canal de Panama collapsed.* But so

---

* *The American government eventually took over the concession. President Theodore Roosevelt detached Panama from Colombia and assigned the Army Corps of Engineers, under General George Goethals, to cut a lock canal. The yellow fever problem was analyzed and overcome, and the project completed. T.R. was always embarrassed about seizing Panama, and launched into a defense of the business whenever it occurred to him. Once he went through this routine during a Cabinet meeting, ending vehemently with "Have I made my point? Have I justified my position?" Secretary of War Elihu Root, a lawyer, gazed at him sardonically, and replied, "Yes, Mr. President. You defended yourself against a charge of seduction, and proved yourself guilty of rape!"*

The Secretary of the Army, Root's successor, later became the sole shareholder of the Panama Canal Company. In the mid-1950s I worked in his office, and once accompanied him down to the annual meeting of the company to help him cast his solitary vote for the reelection of directors and so forth. I was struck by the neatness of the Canal Company's motto: "The Land Divided, the World United."

many prominent personages and influential journalists had been implicated that the truth only leaked out by slow degrees. Finally, because both Herz and de Reinach were Jewish, *La Libre Parole*, an anti-Semitic newspaper, began to run a series of exposés. De Reinach, blackmailed by Herz, committed suicide, provoking a national sensation, and finally forcing government attention.

The resulting investigation revealed that at least 150 senators and deputies, and almost every major paper in the country, had partaken of the torrent of bribes. Only a third of the money invested had gone into actual excavation; a third had gone into bribery and a third simply wasted. Threats and denunciations flew about the Chamber of Deputies. Over a hundred parliamentarians were brought to trial, but a single poor naif who actually confessed was the only one found guilty. The directors, including de Lesseps himself, now in his dotage, were convicted en masse and sentenced to five years behind bars for their part in this sordid tableau.

But there was a happy twist: on the basis of a legal technicality a higher court quashed the sentences. So all came out for the best, although the shareholders' only dividend was that most elegant of all palindromes: A MAN, A PLAN, A CANAL: PANAMA!

THE FLAMEOUT OF THE
TECHNICAL ANALYSTS

POPULAR SWAMIS ARISE IN THE STOCK MARKET from time to time who claim to be able to foretell what the Dow Jones average will do next, based on the recent movements of the squiggly lines. This is called technical analysis, although, in reality it could scarcely be less "technical." The problem seems to be that about the time the swami has figured everything out and developed a vast following, the market changes character, so that his fall, when it comes, is spectacular.

James Dines was the big name in the 1970s. But in late 1974, right at the bottom of the bear market, he took huge ads proclaiming, THE DINES LETTER HAS NEVER BEEN SO BEARISH. In just over a year the Dow thereupon soared from 600 to 1,000. At about the same time other ads appeared, trumpeting the tidings that THE DINES LETTER FEELS GOLDS ARE ON THE VERGE OF A HISTORIC UPMOVE. The yellow metal had a final kick and then dropped in half.

That about did it for Mr. Dines, who was succeeded as everybody's favorite prophet by Joe Granville. Joe published a subscription service, appeared on TV talk shows, and lectured all over the country. His pronouncements became front-page news, and could move the market by themselves. He announced that he never expected to make another mistake. Then came the great bear market of 1982. Granville commanded his followers to sell out, right at the bottom, below Dow Jones 800, and then to go short. By the end of 1983 the market had soared to 1,300, and many volatile issues had tripled or quadrupled. A subscriber who actually followed this advice would have had trouble paying for the renewal of his subscription.

In mid-1982 came large magazine ads by William Finnegan Associates, a firm of computerized seers in Malibu, California, solemnly assuring the reader, "If you happen to know what the Dow Jones Average will be eighty trading days from now, you could make quite an impression on your friends. Not to mention your banker. Well, you can know." To find out you bought a module for a Hewlett-Packard MP-41 computer, you tapped in certain market data, and the program in the module revealed the market outlook for the following eighty days.

The absolute bottom of the 1982 bear market came on August 13, at 767 on the Dow. Every single day for the next eighty days the William Finnegan Associates program called for a market drop, starting with the first day, which predicted a 7.5 percent decline. Instead, the market ran up to over 1,000 during the period.

Why is technical analysis so difficult, not to say impossible? Perhaps because the technical analysts, like alchemists, seek a simple solution to a problem more complicated than they realize. The stock market is the encephalogram of tens of millions of investors, who transmit their greed and fears to each other through the ticker tape and the media. The rules, if any, by which this movement occurs are as complicated as the human psyche itself. The technical analysts who try to reduce it to an orderly formula often forget that the game is changing continuously. In other words, rather than asking what tomorrow will bring if the future is like the past, one should be asking how the game is changing, and how, therefore, the future will be different from the past.

WHISKEY IN MALI

UNLIKELY AS IT SEEMS FOR A COMPLETELY LAND-locked country, one of Mali's principal exports is fish. In the dry season the River Niger recedes to a comparative trickle in the middle of its broad bed, and the cattle, to drink, have to walk out across the dried-out riverbed to reach the little water that is still flowing. They drop manure on the desiccated mud while ambling out and back. This makes fertilizer for the luxuriant flora that grow in the river when it resumes its flow. That rich growth, in turn, permits an extraordinary proliferation of fish, which are caught and exported.

Twenty years ago Mali, the former French Sudan, was in the full course of socialist euphoria, even though there was little to socialize. In response to almost any question, our commercial attaché would pull down a well-thumbed copy of Waugh's *Black Mischief* and with a delighted laugh say, "It's all right here! Listen to this! . . ." Most of the French entrepreneurs had grown discouraged and moved elsewhere. As a result, government revenues fell precipitously. The new Muslim rulers, needing cash, decided to double the tax on whiskey, which, forbidden by Islam, was almost entirely consumed by foreign unbelievers, notably the French.

This instantly created an active new underground pipeline. Trucks full of whiskey came barreling up from Abidjan, capital of nearby Ivory Coast; a case or two would be lowered to the customs guards at the frontier, and the contraband bottles would rapidly find their way into commercial channels through the public market, or *souk*. Also, tax-free diplomatic purchases of whiskey increased enormously as the foreign official community took care of its remaining friends in the shrinking private sector. As a result, the doubled tax rate, instead of doubling the actual tax collected, resulted in tax receipts roughly falling in half.

In due course* the whole question came to a head. What to do about the unexpected and disappointing fall in whiskey import tax revenues? The city fathers followed the only logical course. They doubled the import tax rate on whiskey yet again. Alas, the revenues dropped to virtually zero.

---

* *New York City went through the identical cycle, increasing cigarette taxes over and over again, while a constantly rising proportion of cigarettes entered the city illegally to escape taxation. Now, half the cigarettes sold in New York arrive untaxed.*

Whiskey in Mali

RICHARD WHITNEY

*I have observed that newspaper publicity is usually
followed by a jail sentence.*
NICK THE GREEK

RICHARD WHITNEY'S FINEST HOUR CAME ON OCTO-
ber 29, 1929, still remembered as Black Thursday. Avalanches of
stocks were being dumped in a frenzy of desperation, regardless
of price. The ticker was running hours late. Many on the floor of
the exchange and legions outside of it did not know if they were
solvent or bankrupt. In the midst of this inferno of misery there
appeared on the trading floor Richard Whitney, acting president of the exchange and preferred floor broker of J.P. Morgan
& Company, a large, patrician figure, impeccably turned out.

Strolling with confident, statuesque dignity from one trading
post to another, Whitney entered a series of massive orders for
leading stocks at prices substantially *above* the latest quotations.
He was acting for a group of banks worried that complete collapse was imminent. By the time he had completed his rounds,
he had injected a quarter of a billion dollars of support for the
harried market. There was a sharp rally at this sign of confidence: RICHARD WHITNEY HALTS STOCK PANIC read a headline on
the following day.

Dick Whitney was a golden boy. One good thing had led to
the next: his respectable Boston family entered him in Groton

School in the days of Rector Endicott Peabody, whose benign but stern Christian eye followed young Dick with approval as he became captain of the baseball team, acting captain of the football team, and a school prefect. Proceeding as a matter of course to Harvard, he rowed on the varsity crew and was elected to the Porcellian Club (from Latin *porcellus*, little pig: it was originally intended that members, in addition to being socially satisfactory, be fond of pork). We hear less of academic distinctions, but in those days they were considered secondary, perhaps even slightly grubby.

In 1912 Richard, newly graduated, bought a seat on the New York Stock Exchange, and in 1916 formed his own firm. Thanks to his reassuring credentials and, no doubt, his self-assured, genial charm, Richard Whitney & Co. became principal brokers for J.P. Morgan & Company. It did no harm that Richard was the brother of a Morgan partner, George, and that his uncle had also been a partner. Having a "seat" on the exchange (actually, having the right to stand there) amounted in those days to joining quite a good club or guild more than actually having a job. Your father got you your seat, and after that, thanks to the fixed commission system and the impossibility of buying and selling stocks except through the exchange, you automatically had a handsome living. The people you dealt with, mostly topped off with straw boater hats with club bands in summer or respectable bowlers in winter, were congenial chaps, and the hours were short enough so that after the close you could easily get to the first tee at Piping Rock in time for a round of golf before sundown. A broker who lived on Long Island might pad down of a morning clad in slippers and dressing gown to his launch: on board, one had breakfast and, assisted by one's valet, changed into business clothes and read the *Journal* before disembarking at the foot of Wall Street. Those who lived out the other way, in New Jersey, if they preferred not to be driven to and fro by their chauffeur, could be wafted through the countryside in a special club car with wicker furniture and assiduous stewards: quite painless. Things were civilized . . . not like what's happened since.

Whitney, now a heavy-set man of medium height, belonged to the Jersey contingent. He raised Ayrshire cattle on his several hundred acres and kept a stable of horses, which he rarely rode, although his wife did—sidesaddle. He was a popular fixture in the upper crust: a respected member of the Links, a steward of the Jockey Club. He ran the annual Essex Fox Hounds meet from a tower in the grandstand on the Schley estate, and was head of the 8:08 A.M. club car.

World War I was quite painless. Richard was not asked to submit to the noise, smells, and second-class associations of existence in the trenches. In September 1917 he received a suitable position in the Food Administration in Washington, and in June of the following year was shipped off, not to the front, but back to New Jersey. After a few months he reappeared on Wall Street.

Handling Morgan's transactions on the floor of the exchange, along with such outside customers as his prosperous neighbors in the country, made for a fine business when the market was active—on the way down as well as up. But that was just income. So to build some real capital, Richard plunged heavily in two commercial fertilizer ventures in Florida: one based on mineral colloids, the other on humus. From 1923 to 1931 he sunk more and more money in them—eventually, a total of $1.5 million. He also acquired a house in town, at 115 East 73rd Street, for $100,000, bought another seat on the exchange for $500,000, and maintained a nice lady friend, discreetly offstage in Baltimore.

All very fine. But there was a problem: he didn't actually possess the necessary funds. To invest in the two sure things in Florida and cover general outlays, Richard had to hit up his brother George—who was coining money as a Morgan partner—for about $1 million in loans, plus an additional quarter of a million from his obliging friend Schley.

Richard Whitney's moment of glory in the tabloids had come on Black Thursday, 1929. The next year he was elected president of the Stock Exchange for the first of four one-year terms, just in time to march straight into the Depression and to fight a losing battle with the government against the whole principle of

regulating the securities business. Those were the days of widespread manipulation, insider "pools," inadequate disclosure of
the facts about new issues of securities, banks acting as stock
underwriters (a practice that led to not a few bankruptcies and
loss of the depositors' money), and undisclosed conflicts of interest. There was virtually no control over the adequacy of a broker's capital to meet his obligations. Still, there was a strong
code of professional honor and responsibility, and if something
went wrong, a gentleman felt obliged to put it right.

Whitney was called before the Senate Banking Committee in
1933 and 1934, in the depths of the Depression. The exchange
lay in the doldrums. Brokerage houses were collapsing right and
left; even his own was only marginally profitable. But not only
did he reject utterly the thought that anything whatever about
the Stock Exchange required change, but he moved over to the
attack, exhorting Washington to straighten things out down
there by balancing the budget and reducing disability payments
to former government employees.

Notwithstanding his strenuous advice, the Glass-Steagall Act
became law in 1933, requiring the separation of investment
firms from commercial banks. Then came legislation requiring
much fuller disclosure of the risk factors in new securities issues.
The next year a new Senate investigation even started poking
into a pool managed by the House of Morgan itself. What cheek!
Whitney was asked to distribute an embarrassing questionnaire
to Stock Exchange members. When he stalled, he was accosted
right in his office by representatives of the Senate committee.
"You gentlemen are making a *great mistake*," he declaimed ear-
nestly: *"The Exchange is a perfect institution."* Unconvinced,
the government responded by creating the Securities and Exchange Commission.

Whitney kept up his splendid way of life during all this. He
liked to assemble ten or fifteen of his younger friends for dinner
at the Links, and then, preceded by a police escort with sirens
wailing, be driven up to the Polo Grounds to see the heavy-
weight fights—from ringside, of course. Afterward, back to the
club for champagne: all smiles, all charm.

In 1935 he was passed over for reelection as president of the exchange, but as a consolation was made a trustee of the Gratuity Fund, which provided pensions for the widows and children of defunct members.

In the meanwhile Whitney's Florida fertilizer propositions had gone sour. Fortunately, though, a new source of profit appeared.

Prohibition was a failure. People were drinking more than ever. Almost worse, to stay in business the rumrunners and gangsters who supplied the speakeasies had to fork over huge bribes to the police and City Hall, which fostered corruption. So Repeal became inevitable. During Prohibition Whitney himself had grown fond of a local clandestine applejack called Jersey Lightning. Why not get ready to go into the business when the time came? Jersey Lightning enjoyed the useful merit, compared to bourbon and Scotch, of being ready to drink not in a number of years but a matter of months. This meant that when Repeal did arrive one could be in operation in no time. And of course less capital had to be tied up in inventory. Whitney and another member of his firm organized a venture called Distilled Liquors Corp., in which they subscribed to more than a million dollars' worth of stock at $15 a share. The company bought up a number of old distilleries in New Jersey and New York. Splendid! But how was he to finance his share of the purchase? He couldn't go back to the Morgan bank, since he had borrowed half a million there in 1931 to pay off an earlier bank loan that had come due. His long-suffering brother George, the Morgan partner, had subsequently been obliged to take over this loan. So instead, Whitney borrowed the money from four Wall Street friends.

Early in 1934, Prohibition having finally been buried, the boom in liquor stocks did indeed materialize. Distilled Liquors roared up to $45 a share. But he didn't sell. He was sure this was only the beginning. Alas, the stock never reached that level again. Jersey Lightning somehow failed to take off. Others had foreseen Repeal. Warehouses in Canada and Scotland were brimming with whiskey and gin to be rushed to parched American customers. The price of drinks declined by half. So to support the price of Distilled Liquors stock and to keep the company going, Whitney had to invest more and more heavily, with money borrowed from Stock Exchange friends. His stature on Wall Street rendered it almost a favor for one of the lesser members to be allowed to provide an accommodation to this splendid, genial figure. For a long time Whitney could quite routinely ask other members for the loan of a hundred thousand, although after some years the honor began to pall.

His brother George, who was later made president of the Morgan Bank, became agitated by what he was hearing. Finally he demanded a list of Richard's assets and liabilities, and in due course loaned him $650,000 to clean everything up. But there were items omitted from the inventory. Whitney had been taking money from his own firm's account; when that ran dry he dipped into the customers' accounts, and after that into the Stock Exchange Gratuity Fund itself. In October 1937 it was discovered that Whitney, as broker and trustee of the fund, had six months previously failed to deliver $625,000 worth of bonds that he had bought for it.

The chief officer of the fund instructed Whitney to make delivery forthwith, plus over $200,000 in cash. Whitney replied that this would take a day, as he was shorthanded. But he didn't have the bonds at all: they were in fact held by a bank as collateral for a loan. So the next day Richard appeared yet again in George's office, pleading for help. Poor George, horrified, borrowed the entire sum from his partner Thomas Lamont, explaining that Richard was in a "jam." Whitney was thus able to make good to the Gratuity Fund. George, in despair, now demanded that Richard get out of business altogether: sell his stock in Distilled Liquors and find someone who would take over Richard Whitney & Co.

But Whitney was riding a tiger. Distilled Liquors Corp. was dying and needed more and more money to survive. Whitney kept up a "float" of a couple of million dollars between late 1937 and early 1938 through 111 different small transactions, borrowing, repaying, and borrowing again. This usually involved his now customary technique of approaching acquaintances or even strangers on the floor of the exchange and asking in his friendly, self-assured way for $100,000. There was a memorable encounter when he tried to extract a quarter of a million from a piratical old short-sale artist, "Sell 'em Ben" Smith, who sardonically inquired what assets the loan was based on. "On my face," Whitney replied. "You're putting a pretty high value on your face," snarled "Sell 'em Ben," turning away.

Everything exploded in February. An S.E.C. questionnaire, of just the type that Whitney had so vehemently resisted several years earlier, revealed that his firm had insufficient capital. This triggered an audit. His incursions into the customers' accounts were soon revealed. In March he was hauled down to the Elizabeth Street Police Station and indicted by District Attorney Thomas E. Dewey, soon to be a presidential candidate. A few days later the attorney general of the state accused him of misappropriating funds from the New York Yacht Club, of which he was treasurer. (The Commodore, Whitney's friend Winthrop Aldrich, asked in Newport if he was shocked at the loss of the club's endowment, replied, "I'm disconcerted.") Whitney's firm had already been suspended from the exchange; now the former president and spokesman was personally expelled. Bankruptcy and criminal charges* followed. He was $6 million in the hole. The partners lost everything, or almost: you were entitled in those days to keep two suits. The customers lost whatever they had confided to the firm (although at least one of them got some money back from the exchange itself on the grounds that it had exercised inadequate supervision). The firm's young floor partner Edwin Morgan (no kin to J.P.) never forgave George Whit-

---

* I grew up at 113 East 73rd Street, next door to the Whitneys' house at number 115. One morning, setting forth to school around the block on 74th Street, I encountered a half-moon of reporters lining the sidewalk facing the house. As I halted to take in this development, an impressively turned out Mr. Whitney, complete with bowler hat and sustained by a detective at each side, trotted down the steps of number 115 and into a waiting sedan, as the flashbulbs exploded. Off he went to Sing Sing. Next morning some of the newspaper shots of this great event showed, down in the lower left corner of the picture, a small, pale, ectoplasmic blob. It was the present chronicler, in his first brush with high finance.

ney for not telling him what was going on. By 1937 it was too late, but a few years earlier they could have moved to save the situation.

A whole generation was staggered by Whitney's fall. Most of his friends could scarcely believe it was possible. The grief and disappointment was like that caused to the next generation by the discovery that Alger Hiss was a Russian spy.

At Sing Sing Dick soon became as confident, successful, and popular as ever. He was said to be the only inmate ever called Mr. by fellow prisoners and wardens alike. He was given a soft job in the library. It didn't take him long to be elected captain of the baseball team. By and by Rector Peabody, his old mentor at Groton, paid a call to urge him to profit from this period of immobilization to reflect on the past and learn from his experiences.

"And is there anything that you need, dear boy?" inquired the saint solicitously, thinking, no doubt, of *Pilgrim's Progress* or a hymnal.

Whitney reflected. "Why, yes, sir," he replied. "Do you think you could get me a left-handed baseball mitt?"

THE SOUTH SEA BUBBLE

WE TALK MUCH OF THE INDUSTRIAL REVOLUTION, in which natural instead of human energy was harnessed to tools that operated on an industrial rather than artisanal scale. Often, however, we forget what might be called the Entrepreneurial Revolution. In this the invention of the joint stock company or corporation, an enterprise owned by many participants and with freely transferable shares, played a large part. Toward the end of the seventeenth century the English began to view owning wealth in joint stock company shares as more convenient in many ways than the traditional holding of land—much as we view the situation today.

Agricultural land requires constant, skilled attention. If you buy stock in a large corporation with a history of profitable operations and run by dedicated management, you are not expected to intervene personally. Then, common stock dividends were not taxed (and indeed logically should not be, if the company has already paid tax at the corporate level). And a portfolio of securities is much easier than a farm to divide up among a group of heirs. Particularly, ownership through common stock makes possible the financing of an enterprise on whatever scale its nature may require, which may well exceed the means of a family or partnership. In mounting large industrial undertakings or overseas developments a division of the burdens and the rewards among many broad shoulders presents great advantages.

England had created over one hundred of these companies by the end of the seventeenth century, for banking and insurance, for expeditions, for industrial projects, and to exploit patents, which started to be taken out more freely at that time.

Most wealth still derived ultimately from land, and the high fertility of agriculture in southern climates made such areas as the Caribbean islands and parts of Central America of particular value. Not only are the yields per acre far higher than in England, with its weak sunshine and limited growing season, but spices and fruits proliferate that in England cannot be grown at all. So subtropical agriculture assumed some of the same investment importance that we assign to oil fields. Public interest in Western Hemisphere plantations was whetted by such successes as Sir William Phipps' expedition to the West Indies, which returned its backers a profit of 4,700 percent.

After the defeat of Louis XIV by Marlborough, Spain became England's great commercial rival. The Peace of Utrecht in 1713, which ended the War of the Spanish Succession, opened the Caribbean, Central America, and the northern part of South America to British mercantile undertakings.

The British were groaning under the huge national debt incurred to pay for the French war. The landed gentry and nobility, who had great political influence, loathed this debt, which they saw as a mortgage on landed property—their property. This debt existed in two forms: annuities, typically for a period of ninety-nine years, and bonds, usually bearing interest at 5 percent. The bonds were being paid off progressively. It was the annuities that most vexed the landed proprietors, since having been issued in troubled times they provided an abnormally high return, and could not be redeemed without the holders' consent.

Somehow, the annuitant had to be coaxed out of his shell. So when in 1711 a proposal was put forth to convert some 6 percent government debt into stock in a monopoly company to trade with the Caribbean, Spanish America, and the Pacific Islands, collectively called the South Seas, there was widespread enthusiasm. The necessary legislation was rapidly enacted. The South Sea Company, having taken over £10 million of government debt, in return received this monopoly, plus an annual subsidy from the government.

The first Court of Directors was convened in September, composed of thirty-three members. None had any knowledge of Spanish America or its commerce. Still, thanks to carefully planted rumors, newspaper publicity, and bribes in high places, the company succeeded in conveying an impression of present prosperity and wondrous prospects.

In 1719 the company proposed, in essence, to offer its stock to the public in exchange for the remaining government debt if the government in turn would grant it various further subsidies and concessions. The government was delighted. It had been looking with keen interest across the channel at John Law's machinations in France. Lord Stair, the British ambassador, wrote, "By the success of Mr. Law's project the public debts of France are paid off at a stroke, and the French king remains master of an immense revenue and credit without bounds."

The hidden thought of the company's managers, however, was that if by whipping up speculative interest in the company's stock they could drive up the market price, they could offer less and less of their stock in exchange for any given amount of debt, since debtholders would be able to convert and sell out for an immediate profit. Meanwhile, the managers could keep the excess stock that they had been allowed to create.

That was exactly what happened. The House of Commons accepted the deal on February 2, 1720, and South Sea Company stock forthwith jumped from 129 to 160. When the Lords also agreed, it climbed to 390. "South Sea is all the talk and fashion," wrote a Mrs. Wyndham. "The ladies sell their jewels to buy." Even Isaac Newton succumbed. Originally he bought £7,000 worth of stock, which he sold for twice his cost. He could calculate the motion of the heavenly bodies, he declared, but not the madness of the people. Too true! Seized himself by the same madness that gripped the crowd, he bought back in on a larger scale, and eventually succeeded in losing £20,000.

The company had a limited time to conduct its conversion, so every few weeks new issues of stock were floated, to be paid for with small amounts down and the balance over time. The king himself, who had become Governor of the company, subscribed. In April a 10 percent dividend was declared, payable in stock. The price advanced to 400.

In May the company announced the terms of the first debt-conversion offer directly to the public. For one week, those who submitted their annuities for exchange would receive the equivalent of 375 in South Sea Company stock. By the fifth day the stock had been manipulated up to 495, and the offer became hard to resist. More than half the annuities were exchanged.

By June, thanks to skilled financial moves, an unremitting barrage of propaganda, and the madness of the speculative fever, the stock reached 890.

The "bubble" mania now metastasized. Hundreds of new schemes, seeking over £200 million, were floated, some rational, many not. "For furnishing funerals to any part of Great Britain"; "For trading in hair"; "For a wheel for perpetual motion"; "For assuring seamen's wages"; "For insuring and increasing children's fortunes"; "For the transmutation of quicksilver into a malleable fine metal." Puckles' Machine Company was to revolutionize warfare by firing square shot.

The most notorious bubble company was launched by a promoter who took an office in Cornhill and announced the formation of "a company for carrying on an undertaking of great advantage, but nobody to know what it is." Shares cost £100, and were entitled to a profit of 100 percent per annum. Subscribers made an initial down payment of £2 per share, with the remaining £98 to follow in a month, after the particulars of the business had been announced. This absurd proposition attracted subscriptions—and down payments—for 1,000 shares in a single day. All these flotations of course soaked up a lot of investment demand.

In June the South Sea Company made a £5 million stock

offer for cash, at a price of £1,000. Only a tenth of the subscription was due at once, with the next tenth more than a year later and the remaining eight installments over another four years. Half the House of Lords and the House of Commons subscribed.

The insiders and some of the better-advised speculators, who could understand what was happening, sold. The Canton of Berne caught almost the exact top, clearing £2 million on an original investment of £200,000.

As the succession of conversion offers and cash subscriptions continued, the market became tired. In August the Court of Directors proposed a dividend of 30 percent for the year, and not less than 50 percent for the next ten years. This was to support the stock price at close to its then level by assuring a satisfactory yield—the last concern of the speculators who had bought only a few months before, when vast capital gains had been the expectation. The stratagem failed. The stock faltered. It declined. It began to sink, faster and faster. Greed suddenly turned to fear, and fear to desperation.

By November South Sea stock had collapsed to 135. So many expectations, so many obligations, so much credit had been built upon the structure, that its collapse profoundly shook British finance and business.

King George I, who had remained Governor of the company, returned early from his vacation in his native Hanover. In December Parliament was called into session. Someone had to be responsible; someone should be punished. Lord Molesworth urged that the malefactors be tied in sacks and drowned in the Thames. Nobody dared observe that the speculators themselves, by their lust for profit and their abandonment of common sense, had infallibly brought about their own fate. No, there had to be scapegoats.

Parliament appointed a committee to investigate, which after some months reported that to push the legislation creating the company, free stock had been handed out to influential persons, including Charles Stanhope, a Treasury commissioner, the Earl of Sunderland, and James Craggs the elder and the younger, joint Postmaster-General and Secretary of State respectively.

The Chancellor of the Exchequer, John Aislabie, had received about £800,000, an immense sum in the eighteenth century. In the resulting trial, only Aislabie was convicted—of "notorious, dangerous and infamous" corruption—and imprisoned, but under the South Sea Sufferers' Bill over £2 million was recovered from the directors, whose estates were confiscated.

In addition, those who had borrowed money from the company on the security of stock—including 138 members of the House of Commons—were relieved of this obligation if they paid off 5 percent of the loan. The annuitants who had lost their income recovered about half their loss.

The treasurer of the company, Robert Knight, who knew all its secrets, escaped in disguise by boat to the Continent, taking his papers. Arrested in Flanders, he demanded trial there instead of England. He escaped to France before the jurisdictional conflict could be resolved.

The fine new six-million dollar Sydney
Opera House

THE FINE NEW $6 MILLION
SYDNEY OPERA HOUSE

QUEEN ELIZABETH II OPENED THE SYDNEY OPERA House on October 20, 1973, as sixty thousand balloons rose into a sky rent by fireworks and tortured by screaming military jets. A thousand liberated pigeons cautiously made their way heavenward amidst the chaos.

The building, sometimes compared to "a nun in a windstorm" for its layers of superimposed triangular roofs, was to cost $6 million.

Unfortunately, what with problems over the famous roof, extensive changes in the interior, and other odds and ends, the actual cost came to about $100 million.

The altered interior has, unfortunately, provoked many complaints. The acoustics are poor, not a desirable characteristic in an opera house. The seats are cramped; visibility is spotty. Costs are so high that the operation loses around $10 million a year.

So the prime minister of New South Wales, where Sydney is located, now proposes to change the interior back to the original design.

That little job, it is estimated, will come to $400 million at today's prices. So the Opera House will have cost not $6 million but half a billion, quite aside from the operating losses. Of course, the $400 million price for changing back the interior may itself have been underestimated.

THE PUTREFACTION OF JUAN MARCH,
or,
HOW TO STEAL A COMPANY FOR
1¢ ON THE DOLLAR

At ONE TIME A FIFTH OF ALL THE ELECTRICITY IN Spain was produced by a Canadian corporation, Barcelona Traction, Light & Power. It did business there through local operating companies, notably Ebro Irrigation and Power. It was in turn controlled by SOFINA, a major Belgian enterprise.

The company had floated some £8 million in sterling bonds, on which payments were duly made until the Spanish Civil War broke out in 1936. After the war the Franco government, seeking to rebuild Spain's foreign exchange reserves, would not permit the conversion of pesetas into pounds to service this debt, so the bonds fell into arrears.

To clear up the problem, SOFINA, which had ample funds outside of Spain, proposed an arrangement—the so-called Compromise Plan—under which it would take over the sterling debt payments. The plan was offered to the bondholders at a meeting in London, and accepted by a wide majority, although one group, called Fenchurch Nominees, voted against it. In time it emerged that behind Fenchurch was a sinister figure named Juan March (pronounced Mark), who had been buying up Barcelona Traction's sterling bonds.

Even though the Compromise Plan had been accepted, it had

to be approved by Spain's Ministry of Industry and Commerce. Now began a curious struggle. March threw all his influence—which, although shadowy, was immense—*against* permitting interest to be paid on the bonds he had just bought. What was going on?

March, born in 1880 in Majorca, was a frail, pallid young man who wore thick glasses surmounting a beaklike nose. He never went to school, instead working in a grain warehouse and as a longshoreman. At an early age he entered business, dealing in pigs, buying land, and financing the shipping of contraband. He developed a highly lucrative tobacco-smuggling operation between North Africa and Spain, with its own cigarette factories and shipping line, Transmediterrania, which later dominated Spanish traffic in the Mediterranean. In 1911 the government of King Alfonso, in order to collect at least some revenue, granted him a monopoly of Spanish tobacco sales. Even then he continued smuggling on a large scale.

World War I was for March a time of gratifying business opportunities. He devised a highly satisfactory modus vivendi with both sides. German U-boats prowled the Mediterranean, but had trouble refueling and finding fresh food. From the Balearic Islands March supplied their needs, in return for cash and free passage for the vessels carrying his contraband. He also informed German Intelligence of Allied ship movements.

At the same time he had a contract to supply provisions to the British submarine base at Gibraltar, and induced the Admiralty to persuade the French authorities to let him ship tobacco from Algiers, in return for intelligence on German shipping.

Beside collaborating with and betraying both belligerents, he found a way of squeezing the onlookers. From neutral vessels he demanded protection money against submarine attack. Those who refused to pay were fingered to the Germans—for a substantial reward, naturally.

During the war March got control of extensive real estate, acquired sugar refineries, started banks, bought a steamship line, and became the dominant businessman in Majorca.

In the 1920s March, by now called El Yanqui because of his

energy in both legitimate and criminal activities, was in a position to seek overt influence in Spanish political life. He acquired two Madrid daily newspapers, *Las Informaciones* and *La Libertad;* the first was instructed to adopt a conservative and the second a leftist editorial position. Strangely enough, since March was illiterate into his forties, he probably couldn't read the editorials he was paying for. He also made a substantial contribution to the Spanish army newspaper, and a massive donation to the queen, nominally for a children's hospital, although the money may have gone to Paris to redeem some of the royal family's jewels that had been pawned there.

He ran for the Cortes, the Spanish parliament, from his home town in Majorca in 1923, and was swept in, in part thanks to an immense outdoor fiesta that he staged for the citizens immediately before the election. Unhampered by idealistic scruples, March found it easy enough to accommodate himself to the changing governments that ruled unstable Spain in those years. Under Alfonso XIII he got his tobacco concessions and bought his newspapers; starting in 1925 he became a confidant of the new dictator, Primo de Rivera, and established the Banco March chain, which thrives to this day. Primo de Rivera had previously ordered his arrest for smuggling arms to Moorish revolutionaries. March fled over the Pyrenees to France disguised as a priest. In time he patched things up with the Primo de Rivera government and returned to Spain. There, he cornered Catalonia's potash deposits and expanded his shipping, real estate, agricultural, petroleum, and textile interests.

March had his troubles during the Spanish Republic and in 1931 he not only lost both his tobacco monopoly and his seat in the Cortes but was jailed for smuggling. He was also accused of bribery, of using armed thugs to overbear business adversaries, and of framing three men so that they were shot as German spies, a nasty commercial technique. Fortunately, his confinement was painless: a pleasantly furnished suite, with servants and secretaries. From behind bars he directed the campaign that brought the downfall of the government, added three more Madrid dailies to his press empire, and expanded his oil, farming, and minerals interests. His faithful Majorcans even elected him to the Tribunal of Constitutional Guarantees. After eighteen months March's guard, claiming to "feel sorry" for him, drove off with him to Gibraltar. The guard was well rewarded for this gesture, being enabled to retire to Greece.

In later years, when it became fashionable to have been persecuted by the Republicans, March attributed his stooped gait to "all those years in prison."

By now the Spanish Civil War was brewing. The leader of the insurgents, Francisco Franco, was in exile in the Canary Islands. Who sent a transport plane to fly him back? Who provided tens of millions of dollars in financial backing? None other than Juan March, to whom Franco was thus placed forever under obligation—a situation of which March was to make full use.

"Europe, the West, and—why not say it!—Christianity are in this fabulous man's debt for the support he gave it at certain crucial moments," declared Juan Antonio Suances, later Minister of Industry and Commerce.

March sat out the Civil War in a hotel in Rome, pushing Mussolini to send more Italian troops and supplies to Franco. After the Civil War, Franco gave March a virtual monopoly on trade between Britain and Spain; he also organized barter deals with both Hitler and Mussolini.

In World War II, March was back at his old stand as double agent and smuggler. One might cite the seizure in December 1941 of a vessel of March's Transmediterrania Line by the U.S. authorities, on the grounds of exporting prohibited commodities, including parachute silk and radio parts, apparently headed for Germany but shown on the manifest as "ship's stores." (One likes to think of the captain explaining to the customs inspectors what shipboard crisis would call for parachute-jumping.) Five members of the vessel's company were arrested. March, their master, could have assured them that a trip to jail was nothing to worry about—just a step in one's career, in fact. Still, he took pains to preserve his connections with British Intelligence, and was one of six Spaniards to whom the British Embassy in Madrid was instructed to grant asylum on demand.

· · ·

This, then, was the position as World War II drew to a close and March hatched his attack on Barcelona Traction. The reader will recall that his nominees, owning some of the company's British bonds, had voted against the "Compromise Plan" to enable interest payments to resume. The scene now shifts to Madrid, where Minister of Industry and Commerce Suances had to rule on the acceptability of the plan to the Spanish government . . . the same Suances who had once hailed the smuggler-politician as rescuer of "—why not say it!— Christianity." March applied sufficient pressure; the plan was denied approval. The British bondholders now appealed to their government: Surely there could be discreet diplomatic representations? After all, it wasn't a question of pushing the Spanish to relax their exchange controls: SOFINA already had the money available outside Spain to make payments on the bonds.

But March's years of secret contacts—even if as a double agent—with the Admiralty counted for a lot. The bondholders' pleas echoed without response down the corridors of Whitehall.

The situation of the British creditors was now dismal indeed. Their bonds were in default and there seemed no way to improve the position. March allowed them to simmer gloomily for a year or two. Although he maintained palaces in Madrid, Palma, and Biarritz, he transferred his main headquarters to a hotel in Geneva, where he set up shop accompanied by an entourage including a cook, a chauffeur, a doctor, a man of business, and a combination valet and bodyguard—the latter no idle bit of ostentation. Now turning seventy, paler, bald, and more stooped than ever, he sometimes made sorties to the center of town to play dominoes or checkers, his only recreations, but mostly he sat in a corner of his hotel, a large cigar in the wan face behind the thick glasses, smoking and thinking. His two sons, Juan and Bartolome, looked after his Spanish businesses.

In London, the Barcelona Traction sterling bonds slowly drifted lower and lower, to a deep, sad discount from their face value.

After a while March concluded that the time had come for the next move. He had his agents, Fenchurch Nominees, make a public offer for any or all of the more senior of the two sterling issues outstanding. In a few months he had collected a majority of the issue for a very modest investment—£2 million worth at face value, but only a fraction of that in the market.

There was a pause while March digested this transaction. Then he struck.

On February 10, 1948, some indignant capitalists appeared before a dim but earnest judge in the modest town of Reus, seventy-five miles northwest of Barcelona, waving a bunch of the sterling bonds. They were bondholders. They were entitled to interest. Interest was not being paid. Since the government had refused permission, there was no prospect that interest would ever be paid. Ergo, the company was bankrupt. As senior creditors, they demanded possession of their collateral. They just had to have those interest payments, they wailed: "We are driven not by ambition but by the fear of our own putrefaction!"

This was a slight overindulgence in rhetoric. The petitioners were, as the English say, rushing their fences: they had owned their bonds—and then only as front men for March—for barely five days.

Of course, it was not by some caprice of jurisprudence that this particular courtroom in this out-of-the-way town—Reus, of all places—had been the site of the petition. All had been thought out, carefully pondered amidst clouds of Havana cigar smoke in distant Geneva, all fully prepared, including the generous lubrication of the eminent magistrate himself.

Correcto! pronounced the sage jurist, stoutly. You have been wronged, *señores*, grievously abused. Barcelona Traction, that wormy affair, is adjudged bankrupt. Go get it!

In the following days March's agents, armed with the court's decree, grabbed Barcelona Traction's properties throughout Spain. They invaded the offices, expelled the officers and directors, installed themselves at their desks, started giving orders. They found tens of millions in cash in the till, many multiples of what March had spent on his sterling bonds, quite aside from the immense value of the operating assets themselves—a good quarter of a billion dollars.

A vast howl arose from the company's shareholders overseas.

The company's lawyer was stunned: "We prefer not to comment, for the commentary would be so harsh that our self-respect forbids it." Since Barcelona Traction and SOFINA were foreign companies with foreign shareholders, Canada, Belgium, Great Britain, and the United States all protested.

Then, out of the blue, came a salvo of friendly artillery. One Francisco Garcia del Cid slapped a *declinatoria* on the Reus court, challenging its competence in the matter. Quite right! Why Reus, of all places? To be sure, this development did complicate Barcelona Traction's struggle against March in one respect. Until the *declinatoria* was disposed of, any litigation was frozen. That meant, for instance, that Ebro, which was swimming in cash, could not appeal against the bankruptcy judgment. The *declinatoria* remained in effect throughout the weeks in which March was seizing the operating companies. Then Senor Garcia del Cid suddenly withdrew it. Instantly the Reus judge announced that since the time within which any appeal had to be filed had expired, the bankruptcy was now absolute. Garcia del Cid had been yet another Juan March stooge.

In April a special judge was appointed to investigate the whole business. Bang! Another *declinatoria*, this time filed by a certain Juan Boter Vaquer, again, as it emerged, a March creature. This bottled up all legal resistance for yet another eight months.

In May March came up with an offer of settlement. He would give the shareholders of Barcelona Traction £2 million and a quarter-interest in a new company that would take over all the assets of the old one. He, of course, would take the other three-quarters. This outrageous proposal was indignantly rejected.

December 1948 rolled around—time for the annual meeting of the company, held, since Canada was its place of incorporation, in Toronto. Great was the rage of the wretched shareholders, loud their plaints. But nobody could think of anything for them to do except fume.

Eventually the Spanish government yielded to worldwide indignation so far as to permit the formation of a "Commission of Experts" from Spain, Canada, and Britain, to examine whether in the four decades since its incorporation Barcelona Traction had on balance brought money into Spain, which might justify letting the company, notwithstanding exchange control, repatriate enough to pay off its sterling bonds, or whether it had on balance taken money out over the period. The experts split. The Canadians and British concluded that the company had brought in, net, £19 million, while the two Spaniards claimed that millions of pounds had been taken abroad. The final report of the commission reflected only the Spanish view and concluded that the government had been right in refusing to let the company convert pesetas into pounds, and would be right in continuing to refuse in the future. John Balfour, British ambassador in Madrid, signed the Agreed Minute of this commission on instructions from the Treasury—whose motives can be surmised. The motives of Angel Andana Sanz, one of the two Spanish "experts," were quite easy to fathom: he was an ex-employee of Juan March.

This obstacle surmounted, March pressed on. He could not get his hands on the actual stock certificates of Barcelona Traction, so in 1951 new ones were printed. It was declared that they must find a new home before they became "rancid," so they were promptly offered for sale at auction. The only accepted bidder, who thus acquired all the stock of a company worth about $250 million for a mere $280,000, was a previously unknown enterprise called Catalonian Electric . . . owned, it turned out, lock, stock, and barrel by Juan March.

The desperate real owners engaged an in-law of Generalissimo Franco himself to cry for justice, and the year after, in 1954, retained Arthur Dean, a partner of the New York law firm of Sullivan and Cromwell, to argue their claims. Dean did obtain an interview with the Caudillo, who, he reported to his clients, had been gracious enough to intimate that the problem would receive attention. But needless to say, Juan March's claims upon his old friend Franco vastly outweighed any briefs, however tightly drafted, by Messers Sullivan and Cromwell. Indeed, Franco liked the idea of bringing foreign-owned Spanish companies back under Spanish control. How could it be done more cheaply than this? And who could be more worthy than his sometime rescuer, for whom something certainly had to be done?

In Spain March now appeared as the irremovable proprietor of one of the country's leading enterprises, quite aside from his huge accumulation of newspapers and other assets, both officially and sub rosa in Switzerland. As befitted his status, he held a little party back in Majorca for his granddaughter. A thousand workers strung 200,000 lights in his gardens to provide a suitably cheerful tone. It was said that for the occasion he had bought all the flowers on sale in Majorca. The government radio covered the proceedings minute by minute. This social splash did not empty March's exchequer, estimated to be in the low hundreds of millions of dollars in Spain, with immense additional sums salted away in Switzerland.

The faithful old shareholders of Barcelona Traction felt neglected amidst this jollity. In 1958 Belgium, home of SOFINA, which controlled the company, brought suit at the International Court of Justice at The Hague, claiming $140 million from Spain in compensation for stolen assets. For years the case dragged on, filling shelf upon shelf with briefs, documents, and depositions. At one point the matter was voluntarily withdrawn from the court when March offered to pay the full market price for the Barcelona shares. This, however, turned out to mean the price either at the time of the Reus "bankruptcy" or the bogus auction. From $85 in 1928 the shares had collapsed to $3 in those periods, representing a capitalization of $5 million for the whole company, an absurd figure, less than its profit in one good year and only a fraction of its cash in the bank in Spain. So the endless process resumed.

Finally all the arguments had been heard, answered, and rebutted, all the briefs filed, studied, attacked, and defended, all the documents submitted, numbered, and examined. The sixteen judges, not one of whom had been on the bench when the case was originally brought, withdrew to contemplate their verdict. It was a stunner. After eleven years—not months, years!—they declined to rule on the substance of the case at all, invoking the

technical point that Belgium lacked "standing"—was not qualified to sue on behalf of a Canadian company.

The rightful Barcelona Traction issued a lugubrious final report in 1974. With melancholy indignation it observed that "the
shareholders of this company have been deprived of their entire
investment."

So had Juan March. He had perished in 1962 in a car crash
outside Madrid. The newspaper eulogists outdid themselves.
The swindler, double agent, and smuggler was compared to Vir-
gil and extolled as "our Picasso or Rubens of financial art." His
foundation, the most important in the country, formed in 1955
when he was a resident and numbered-account proprietor of
Geneva, flourishes as a monument to his "love for Spain, her national character, and Christian civilization."

AFTERWORD

WHEN LARGE MATTERS GO AWRY, THEY OFTEN follow standard patterns. So perhaps this volume, like a bird-watcher's handbook, will help the reader identify some of the familiar ones—groupthink, hubris–nemesis, the Ponzi scheme, speculative manias, the "distance lends enchantment" mirage, and other raptures—as they occur, alone or in combination.

1. That aspect of the herd instinct sometimes called group-think is one of the strongest forces in life. People will go along with an authoritative leader's crazy decision even though they half-know that they are being led to perdition. They become sleepwalkers.* Groupthink rules the stock market, and one sees it gripping the participants in the speculative frenzies described in these pages. Every experienced person has also encountered groupthink on the committee level. Pearl Harbor was a prodigious example. Not one officer on Admiral Kimmel's staff dared dispute his conviction that the Japanese would not attack the base, even though Washington sent out one war alert after an-

---

* *"I felt I had been carried up into the midst of the air and could hear the earth turning below me," said Napoleon of his time of glory.*

other. So operations were never placed on a war footing and the fleet was destroyed. If an irascible boss holds your career in his hands, it takes courage to contradict him. You'll be odd man out even if the future proves you right.

The convincing, but wrong, idea—the *claire idée fausse*—is an important groupthink variation. Exciting buzzwords and clever slogans often transmit fallacies,* since mankind craves simple solutions to complicated problems. It would not seem premature to include Communism as a *claire idée fausse*. The miseries of stock market "technical analysis" provide a fine example. The Pruitt-Igoe project qualifies, and one sees the principle contributing to the John Law scandal debacle. For one subvariation I've coined the term "Noah's Ark fallacy." This arises when an enthusiastic buyer pays twice book value for shares in the Noah's Ark Shipbuilding Company. He's vainly hoping for a recurrence of a one-time situation, as when Xerox sunk a billion dollars into Scientific Data Systems. S.D.S.'s business had enjoyed an enormous boom furnishing powerful computers to the space program, but having satisfied that demand, they couldn't hope to repeat the sale right away.

2. The classic description of hubris leading to nemesis is *Quem vult perdere deus, prius dementat* ("Whom god would destroy he first drives mad")—with power, typically, the way we often say "*drunk* with power." Pride cometh before a fall. In many of the preceding stories, the protagonist, as in a Greek drama, believing he has become godlike, is undone by hubris: de Lesseps, Ivar Krueger, Richard Whitney, Bernie Cornfeld. A variation is underestimating the opponent. Juan March's victims didn't study his record closely enough to realize his immense ingenuity and utter ruthlessness. Like a prominent mob-connected businessman, his high connections were no indication of respectability; indeed, they made things worse. To save themselves his victims needed to plan their defenses as far ahead as March planned his attack. In the same way many large international companies, responding to Italian government incentives, started

---

* *"It is astonishing what foolish things one can temporarily believe if one thinks too long alone," said John Maynard Keynes.*

factories in Sicily in the 1960s, only to give up when they discovered the full costs of doing business in a Mafia environment. Another invisible opponent that historically has often taken a fearful toll is disease. Soldiers know about it more than financiers. Dysentery killed far more British soldiers in the Crimea than the Turks did; Napoleon's defeat in Russia was due as much to hypothermia as enemy action. Just so with the Compagnie des Indes colonists in Louisiana, and de Lesseps' engineers in Panama.

3. A Ponzi scheme, simply stated, consists of paying off the earlier participants in a bubble with the money of the later ones. Americans encounter it regularly in pyramid clubs and door-to-door-selling organizations of the "Dare to Be Great" variety, in which your payoff comes from recruiting salesmen, who are supposed to recruit still more salesmen, and so on ad infinitum. Something always comes along to break the flow of the endless buildup. You can depend on constant revivals of the Ponzi scheme paradigm. A recent one was called J. David & Co. Mr. David (like Ponzi, this was a *nom de guerre*) had a plan to make your money grow with wondrous speed. First you turned it over to him. Then he embarked on your behalf in great speculations, notably in foreign currencies. You received no detailed reports, just an occasional bulletin reporting how your fortune had grown—20 percent, 50 percent, 100 percent, 200 percent. Of course, currency speculators can't do that well steadily. Both currency and commodity speculators almost always lose their touch (and their money) in due course. And yet J. David was able to collect over $100 million with this flytrap, from people who should have known better. Now the investigators are trying to discover where the funds disappeared to.

4. Speculative manias have Ponzi characteristics, since as prices rise and the mania spreads, more money floods in, putting prices higher than ever. Under the "bigger fool" theory you pay too much, knowing you're a fool, because you hope a bigger fool will pay you still more. The Dutch Tulipomania is the classic example of this genre, but the whole stock exchange occasionally turns into a self-inflicted Ponzi scheme during the blowoff

stage of a boom, when problematic companies sell for fifty times earnings, amidst assurances on every side that "So-and-So can only go up." Listen for those words! They are the trumpets of doom. Students of the cultural anthropology of the stock market will recognize the "New Era" mirage in the Kuwait Stock Exchange story. "This time, things are quite different," the crowd assures itself; the law of gravity is hereby officially suspended, and Fidogenetics or whatever now really is worth three times what anybody had thought. (Then, of course, it collapses.) One would expect the present epidemic of "leveraged buyouts" to grow into such a speculative splurge, like the "hi-tech," conglomerate, and hedge fund fads of the past decade.

5. The "welsher of last resort" problem—of impossibly large government indebtedness, as described in the John Law, South Sea Bubble, and War Loan Conversion chapters—is with us today. A long war or a populist government often semibankrupts a country, so that its creditors, including holders of paper money, cannot be paid. Repudiation is inevitable; the only question is what form it will take. Governments have learned to debauch the currency to get out of debt: where ten marks once bought a pair of shoes, soon it takes a thousand or a million or even a billion. (In the German hyperinflation, it took 40 trillion.) That makes a hundred-billion-mark national debt manageable soon enough. In the eighteenth century, before the popularization of this technique, both France and England succeeded in coaxing the holders of government I.O.U.s into swapping them for shares in El Dorado speculations—the Compagnie des Indes and the South Sea Company. The British devised a neat alternative in this century by appealing to their citizens' patriotism to exchange a mediocre piece of paper for a bad one: the War Loan Conversion.

One wonders what technique will be used to solve today's debt crisis. Few countries can pay the interest, let alone the principal, on their indebtedness. Even America's national debt now equals the value of all the companies on the stock exchange, and its interest equals our budget deficit. So really we are printing money to pay the interest, like any Third World country. Eventually, something will snap. The eighteenth-century solution of an officially sponsored company whose shares can be paid for with wormy government paper might work again abroad. It could be a huge holding company of shares in nationalized industries. I hereby offer the idea, gratis, to Mexico, Brazil, and Argentina.

Felix Rohatyn and others suggest that governments should guarantee and stretch out international debt at much lower interest rates than those now prevailing. This would enable the inevitable repudiation in real terms to occur gently by letting inflation accomplish its mighty working over time. Perhaps a future version of this volume will include the then former Secretary of the Treasury Rohatyn together with sometime Chancellor of the Exchequer Neville Chamberlain among the high priests of finance who administered ritual euthanasia to intractable public indebtedness.

6. A category of folly that recurs endlessly can be styled the "distance lends enchantment to the view" paradigm. One blithely embarks on projects in faraway lands that one would shun at home where one understood the hazards: de Lesseps' catastrophe in Panama, the Groundnuts Scheme, the South Sea Bubble, the Compagnie des Indes. The Scottish colonization of Darien, in Central America, during the last years of the seventeenth century, was another grim story of this type. The entire project came to nothing; of the thousands of settlers only a handful survived.

In our own day, prosperous citizen D. K. Ludwig plunged a cool billion into his plan to raze the forests of northern Brazil and substitute more productive varieties of agriculture. He was laid low not only by the physical problems of the venture, but by that Latin American specialty, the predatory politician, who has taken over the function previously filled by the anopheles mosquito. A recent "distance lends enchantment" fiasco was Adela, a venture-capital company conceived by Senator Jacob Javits and hatched by a large group of splendid international banks and industrial companies—Citicorp, Exxon, Philips Lamp, and the like—to show the world how one could make

money in Latin America. It opened offices in all the Latin
American capitals, and hired green business-school graduates to
spread its funds among hundreds of ventures. In spite of the high
sponsorship and the ever-enthusiastic reports of President Ernst
Keller, the shareholders' money was lost. Adela's lamentable
story needs to be written, and I commend it to Ph.D. candidates.

7. Invincible Ignorance is perhaps the name for the misplaced government interventions recounted in "Whiskey in
Mali," as well as those of the French revolutionary hyperinflation. Now that we no longer read history we have only recent
experience to learn from. We can see a similar folly devastating
my own city, New York, in the form of permanent rent control.
Every observer knows what rent control does to a big city: it in-
duces low-skilled people to remain where there are few low-
skilled jobs, which forces the highly skilled people to live far
away or perhaps leave. Then you bankrupt the landlords, often
persons of modest means themselves, so that the buildings can't
be maintained, and eventually are lost. Mile upon mile of Har-
lem and the South Bronx have been burned out, like German
cities in World War II, except that we have done it to ourselves.
That, of course, shrinks the housing supply, raising housing
costs. Do the politicians understand this fatal process? Perfectly.
Do they espouse rent control to get elected? Of course. When
special interests get strong enough to control decision-making,
sound government becomes impossible.

Invincible Ignorance is overcome when its price is seared into
the national consciousness with a branding iron. Ever since the
hyperinflation of the Weimar Republic and its disastrous consequences, including, indirectly, Hitler, the Germans have
watched over the soundness of their currency, just as we stretch
"safety nets" to ward off a repetition of the 1930s Depression.
Italy may be relatively safe from counterproductive price controls, since they form the central episode in the greatest Italian
prose work of the nineteenth century, which every Italian
schoolchild almost memorizes, Manzoni's *I Promessi Sposi* (*The
Betrothed*). As inflation, in the novel, rages on, the authorities
decree longer and longer periods of imprisonment in chains or

forced service in the galleys for infractions of price controls, but no measure has any effect. As one sees in the present volume's chapter on the French Revolutionary hyperinflation, once "funny money" comes in, no amount of regulation can hold prices down. Perhaps some modern-day Manzoni will save New York by writing honestly of the fatal consequences of rent control plus "welfare." Alas, it seems unlikely. My writer friends are solidly dug into rent-controlled apartments themselves and are charmed by that arrangement.

The syndrome that begets inflation and then unavailing price controls seems as old as history. Hammurabi's code in about 1745 B.C. and Diocletian's in A.D. 301 attempted minute regulation of prices. Hammurabi prescribed execution (apparently by drowning) for merchants who demanded payment in silver; so did the Directory, during the French hyperinflation. Diocletian's code specified the price of each quality of shirt, as, unavailingly, did our Office of Price Administration in World War II. But suppressing the symptoms doesn't halt the disease. The price of wheat rose over one hundred times between Augustus and Diocletian's code; far from being arrested, in the next generation it rose about a thousandfold. So why, after all these millennia, do we still treat inflation by controlling prices instead of government expenses and the money supply? Invincible Ignorance. *"Semper vult mundus decipi: decipietur,"* said the Swedish chancellor Oxenstierna: "The world always wishes to be deceived: let it be deceived."